# SOLVING PARTNER-LEVEL CHALLENGES

This publication is designed to provide accurate and authoritative information on the subject covered. It is sold with the understanding that the publisher is not engaged in rendering legal service. If legal advice is required, the services of a competent professional should be sought.

©Advisory Publications, 2001. Copyright strictly reserved.
This book may not be reproduced in whole or part without the written permission of Advisory Publications.

# *Table of Contents*

## Chapter 1: Nine Rules for Group Success .................. 5
Remember These Helpful Principles .......................................... 6

## Chapter 2: Promoting to Partnership ........................... 9
Consider Economic Indicators —
Offer Buy-in to the Right Person .......................................... 10
Who Should Become Your Partner? ....................................... 11
Future Promises for New Physicians ..................................... 15
New Partner Arrangements .................................................. 16
Consider 'Part-time' Partner Arrangements ........................... 17
Decouple the Buy-in Arrangements ....................................... 21
Computing the Stock Purchase Price on Net Book Value ...... 23
Structuring the Buy-In for a High Value Practice ................... 25
Special Situations in New Partner Buy-ins ............................. 27

## Chapter 3: Physician Leadership ................................ 29
The Critical Success Factor .................................................... 30
Addressing Business Planning ................................................ 32
Developing Leadership in Your Group ................................... 34
It's Not a Kingship ................................................................. 37
Business Training for Physicians ............................................ 38
Enable Your Managing Physician to Perform ........................ 39
Pay for Valuable Leadership .................................................. 41
Guidelines for Defining Physician-Leader Compensation ...... 42

## Chapter 4: Group Governance ..................................... 45
Working Toward the Good of the Group ............................... 46
Require Non-Clinical Training for *All* Group Members ......... 48
Governance Issues in Everyday Practice ................................ 51
Develop a 'Best-of-Class' Attitude .......................................... 53
Evaluate Your Partners — and Yourself ................................. 54
Sample Physician Evaluation Form ........................................ 56

## Chapter 5: Dealing with Problem Partners ................. 57
Protect the Group Against Its Partners — Not Vice Versa ...... 58
Review Your Partner Arrangements ....................................... 59
Address Behavioral Handicaps ............................................... 61
Impose Sanctions for Continuing Problems ........................... 63
How — and How Much — Can You Penalize a Non-compliant Partner? ... 64
When All Else Fails, Vote to Expel ......................................... 67
Assessing Medicare Fines After a Partner's Departure ........... 67

## Chapter 6: Partner Compensation ............................................. 71
Adapt Your Formula to Meet Practice Goals ............................................ 72
Face it Now: One Group's Experience ..................................................... 74
Compensation Concepts ............................................................................ 75
Simplify Your Compensation Approach ................................................... 77
Track RVU Production for Income Division ............................................ 79
Managed Care Still Weighs In ................................................................... 80
Try Three Tiers First .................................................................................. 83
Special Situations Require Special Formulas ........................................... 84
How to Handle Compensation Questions
   When a Partner Wants to Cut Back ....................................................... 87
Paying Partners for Taking on Extra Duties ............................................. 88
An Online Tool to Help Evaluate Your Physician Pay Plan ..................... 90

## Chapter 7: Legal Issues ....................................................... 93
New Stark II Revision Finally Clears Up Major Questions ..................... 94
*Designated health services (DHSs)* ........................................................ 95
Defining a 'Group' ..................................................................................... 95
Sharing the Profits .................................................................................... 96
*Sample Stark-compliant formula calculation* ......................................... 97
Address Partners' Conflicts of Interest ..................................................... 98
Up Front, Not Under the Table ................................................................ 100
Final Stark II Designated Health Services Definitions and Exemptions ... 101
*Criteria for determining if a service qualifies*
   *under the in-office ancillary services exemption* .............................. 102

## Chapter 8: Arrangements for Departing Members ..... 103
Include Provisions for the Good of the Departing Member
   and the Group .................................................................................... 104
Restrictive Covenants .............................................................................. 106
Are Restrictive Covenants Enforceable? ................................................. 108
Partial Retirement ................................................................................... 110
Full Retirement or Other Departure ....................................................... 113
Defining Goodwill .................................................................................... 114
General Benchmarks for Goodwill Values .............................................. 115
Calculating 'Going Concern' Value ......................................................... 116
The More Things Change ........................................................................ 117
Advance Provisions for Special Situations ............................................. 121

## Acknowledgements ............................................................ 124

# Chapter 1

*Nine Rules for Group Success*

## Remember These Helpful Principles

Contrary to popular belief, a six-doctor group practice is *not* six solo practices sharing office space. As practices grow in number of physicians, partners face issues that simply never arise in smaller settings and encounter many difficulties relating to how they apply the basic rules of organizational success.

Disaster is right around the corner when group members hold on to ideas and ideals that have outlived their usefulness. Law firm consultant Milton Zwicker lists the six most common misperceptions about group practice. While he writes with law firms in mind, they apply strikingly well to medical groups, as well. So here are the *myths* (restated to medical practice), for your thought:

- *To get patients, you only need to do good work.*
- *Democracy is the best form of governing the group.*
- *With enough time and meetings, the best management decisions occur by consensus.*
- *Every associate becomes a partner.*
- *A partnership is forever.*
- *Seniority is the appropriate way to divide group income.*

We confront these myths of group practice in this book, advising you how to make effective group decisions, select new partners, divide income fairly and lay the groundwork for graceful departures. The advice you'll find is grounded in nine rules for group success:

***1.*** *Partners must be accountable to the group.* Each physician-member must work for the group's overall success, not just his/her own standing. Managed care and a constantly evolving health care environment require team play.

***2.*** *Partners must share basic goals and philosophies.* Even if diverse in clinical expertise and individual personality, your members have to be on the same page when it comes to important group tenets. If not, you risk partner defections and, possibly worse, internal gridlock when trying to form and carry out important strategies.

***3.*** *A fair amount of trust must exist among partners.* Unless each member feels that his or her partners are working in the practice's best interests, you'll encounter harmful dissension at critical times.

***4.*** *Strategic planning is essential.* You can no longer go along with the idea that just practicing good medicine ensures success. The group must have an identified plan for how to proceed in a more business-oriented health care scene than in the past.

***5.*** *Compensation is the ultimate tool, setting the tone for practice.* Pay and management go hand-in-hand. People, physicians included, tend to work towards goals for which they have an incentive. Whatever your strategic plan, it won't succeed if compensation policy is contrary to its objectives.

***6.*** *Profitability is essential.* Even in specialties with declines in income, if your group is doing worse than most you'll find it difficult to keep members committed to practice goals.

***7.*** *A group needs centralized management.* It's nice to think that, as partners, all members can participate in business and management decisions, but life doesn't work that way. Fully democratic groups flounder. They simply can't make important decisions quickly enough in a demanding business environment.

**8.** *Leaders must stay involved in management.* The top physician-officers can't ignore how non-doctor administrators perform. Good physician-leaders keep a group on track by overseeing and directing their managers.

**9.** *Values must be consistent.* We can't make this point strongly enough. If your partners aren't on basically the same ethical, philosophical and moral wavelength, you'll have trouble taking important actions.

By conducting your medical practice in line with these principles, you can focus on the truly difficult challenge of continuing to provide the best quality care to your patients in these stressful times.

# Chapter 2

*Promoting to Partnership*

## Consider Economic Indicators — Offer Buy-in to the Right Person

Despite the growing market penetration and perceived threat of managed care, the co-ownership arrangements that became customary during the 1980s — the so-called golden age of private practice — prevailed into the early 1990s. Those arrangements called for virtually every new associate physician to become a co-owner after a brief two- to three- year trial period, and then for the young partner to earn the right to a full income share after four or fewer years of co-ownership.

Times have changed and often practices feel pressured to rush advancement to partner status. We maintain that it behooves practice leaders to take their time when possible, making sure a potential partner fits, and to frequently review buy-in agreements, which outdate rapidly.

### Economic factors prevailed

The most significant factor was, of course, fear of reduced incomes. Physicians became loathe to bring on a new doctor moving toward equal income sharing if the practice wasn't growing to support the extra share.

The emergence of eager medical practice purchasers, like physician practice management companies (PPMCs) and hospital systems, made doctors wary. Competition to buy practices inflated their values, compared to previously common doctor-to-doctor sales.

For some, the temptation to sell was strong. Owners became understandably reluctant to invite new members who might dilute the profits. Advisors urged practice owners to consider this factor in structuring new-doctor arrangements.

Today, prospects of future financial success are at best mixed and PPMCs on the decline. Groups are faced with many of the same partnership structure issues they faced 15 years ago. The idea of "partnership" remains uppermost in independent practices and a key recruitment factor in many specialties.

**Invite the right associates into co-ownership**

Partners intent on staying independent must still offer new physicians the opportunity to become co-owners. Adding new partners clearly holds value. A sequence in physician-owners' ages best serves a practice, allowing the mantle of leadership to be passed on without major disruption. And partnership may best promote real understanding and involvement in a practice's business.

*But not every associate should become a co-owner.* Bringing excellent clinical skills to the practice should not by itself justify becoming a partner. The stakes are too high these days for pure clinicians to make (or even to heavily influence) critical business decisions.

The better view is that new co-owners must contribute more to the practice than just the ability to take good care of patients. Those additional factors, of which executive leadership and business management are two examples, depend on the specific circumstances of the practice. When a new physician meets those qualifications, be pleased to invite him or her into co-ownership.

Following the suggestions in this chapter will obviously keep some physicians from becoming partners. We admit this advice is not often followed and is sometimes risky. Treat these non-owners fairly from an income standpoint, for they remain important to the group. Despite managed care, patients still establish relationships with individual doctors; undue physician turnover does not serve a practice well.

# Who Should Become Your Partner?

Employing a young associate does not commit you to making him or her your partner. Although we've espoused that philosophy for more than a decade, only in the last couple of years is it being given more than lip-service. Changes in the economics of medical practice now make our long-standing advice cutting-edge: Be extremely critical before bringing someone into co-ownership.

Nevertheless, many physicians still think that an associate should automatically become a partner after the initial one to three years of employment. That attitude derives from the respect young and old physicians have for each other, taking into account that the younger doctors may even be better trained. And it is fueled by discussing, and even agreeing upon, the basic arrangements before young doctors come to work.

More often than not, though, casually promoting to partner status comes from physicians' unwillingness to face a very critical decision: Does the young doctor have what it takes be a partner in your practice? Not all do, as we discuss in more detail below.

### Critically evaluate every potential partner

Because not every associate will make a good partner, be extremely critical before promoting to co-owner status. We have seen too many mismatches, embarrassments and messy partner-level split-ups among ill-chosen members. Life's too short for such difficulties! *If any doubt exists, do not offer the promotion.*

Your employment contract with the young doctor hopefully allows you to decide whether or not to proceed to partnership. The idea of both sides making a critical evaluation is thus implicit in your relationship. You're under no obligation to promote your associate unless you truly want him/her as your partner for the rest of your practice life.

An unwillingness to critically consider if your associate is partner material may indicate you're not facing up to a few even more basic questions:

- ✓ *What should it mean to be a partner?*

- ✓ *Is a partner simply a good doctor who has stayed with you for a few years?*

- ✓ *Or is a partner someone who exhibits those business, entrepreneurial or other special capacities that help the group continue to prosper?*

Before promising partnership path to a new recruit, define the minimum obligations of being a co-owner and measure new recruits against them. You'll also want to encourage all current co-owners to measure up to these standards. Three features that must be on any group's list are:

- *Setting the quality standard.* While every physician in the group must be clinically reliable, partners practice at the forefront. They should perform a cut above the others, intolerant of less than excellent quality. Despite economic pressures, the game is still won or lost on quality; you can't let any element distract the group from this point.

- *Entrepreneurial contribution.* Every partner owes the group his/her active participation in its management in one form or another. Beyond that, being a co-owner also means accepting ownership's risks along with its rewards. A doctor simply wanting to practice good medicine for an assured income should remain an employee, not an owner.

- *Personal contribution.* A partner must clearly add value to your organization by his/her work product. That may be in production of revenue or in other areas that make the group more successful. Co-ownership demands more time, energy and commitment than expected of an employee.

## Medical practice is a business

Unfortunately, doctors rarely appreciate why their group members serve as partners or what responsibilities they should assume. Compared to commercial business, professional service groups traditionally have one serious problem: The owners/executives are also the hands-on income producers.

In commercial companies, the owners and executives run the business while machines and/or employees produce the goods. Medical practices must begin to recognize the need for owner/executive ability versus producer capabilities. Hence a partner *must* bring value to the practice as an executive or possessor of some other skill(s) of special value to the enterprise.

A young doctor may or may not be partnership material even if s/he possesses superb clinical skills and produces revenue. A group definitely needs such workers and should pay them generously, but that effort alone does not necessarily make them good candidates for partnership. Law, accounting and architectural firms function that way; medical groups should, as well.

## How long the wait?

Our own ongoing reader surveys reveal that the tradition of promising early partnership to new associates lives on in most specialties. The promises show up in new-doctor contracts stipulating when the group will promote to co-owner or partner.

The table on the next page from our most recent reader survey breaks out the percentage of each hiring specialty promising partnership and how long, on average, new associates must wait.

Most practices require a new physician to put in about two years before achieving partnership — not long enough, in our opinion. It's fine to promise you'll *consider* making a good young associate your partner, but some contracts flat out guarantee it. And they promise partnership based solely on time employed, not necessarily on performance or fit with the practice.

Don't be pressured by young candidates' expectations. In many specialties — except primary care — there's a fair supply of young candidates today, so don't rush to fill a vacancy. It's more important to ensure your new associate really qualifies to be your partner.

## Make the tough decision

It's both uncomfortable and stressful to turn down a young fellow-professional after working side-by-side for several years. It's even worse, though, to end up with the wrong partner. Facing up to this difficult, critical decision protects you from the latter fate.

Turning away a marginally satisfactory young doctor is far better than promoting someone who won't strengthen the practice. Or you might have to insist that s/he put in another year or two as an associate. You could also offer an alternative non-ownership arrangement.

Promoting only those physicians with the needed ownership and entrepreneurial skills solves the problem of having unsatisfactory co-owners. Yet it creates another problem: If clinically qualified young doctors are denied traditionally important status, how do you retain them as employees?

## Golden handcuffs retain good clinicians

The answer lies in what we call "golden handcuffs." If you meet a capable physician-employee's financial expectations, there may be less incentive to go elsewhere. Make a permanent associate's salary generous, though obviously less than that earned by the partners.

## Future Promises for New Physicians

| Specialty: | % of Hiring Practices Promising Partnership | Average No. Years Before Partnership | % of Hiring Practices Requiring Restrictive Covenant |
|---|---|---|---|
| **Primary Care:** | | | |
| Family Practice | 30.4% | 1.3 | 82.6% |
| Internal Medicine | 40.0% | 1.4 | 80.0% |
| Pediatrics | 77.3% | 2.5 | 77.3% |
| **P.C. Surgical:** | | | |
| Ob-Gyn | 84.2% | 2.4 | 73.7% |
| Ophthalmology | 33.3% | 1.0 | 18.8% |
| ENT | 100.0% | 2.6 | 31.8% |
| **Spec. Int. Med.:** | | | |
| Neurology | 66.7% | 1.8 | 42.9% |
| Hem/Onc | 100.0% | 2.0 | 33.3% |
| Nephrology | 100.0% | 1.8 | 100.0% |
| Pulmonology[1] | 66.7% | 2.0 | 66.7% |
| Gastroenterology | 100.0% | 2.4 | 100.0% |
| Cardiology | 100.0% | 2.4 | 68.4% |
| **Surg. Specialties:** | | | |
| Gen/Vasc Surgery | 100.0% | 2.1 | 75.0% |
| Neurosurgery | 66.7% | 1.8 | 100.0% |
| Orthopedics | 100.0% | 1.8 | 81.3% |
| Urology | 100.0% | 2.5 | 88.9% |
| **Dermatology:** | 40.0% | 1.3 | 40.0% |
| **Anesthesiology:** | 100.0% | 2.0 | 75.0% |
| **Overall:**[2] | 72.5% | 1.9 | 76.9% |

**Notes:**
[1] Sample size is less than 5 practices.
[2] Overall figures include multispecialty practices and specialties with sample sizes less than 3.

Consider a special incentive program to help instill a sense of partnership without the economic risks or management burdens assumed by partners. Provide such long-term associates, or members, with incentives in their own profit centers. This allows still more potential profit for the actual partners.

Adopt this process only after you critically evaluate the partnership concept. A partner's share of income consists of two elements that are at least theoretically separate in medical practice corporations:

- Income from actual work providing medical services
- Return on the ownership and management of a profitable activity

In specialties with physician oversupply, many more doctors are satisfied to remain as well-paid employees than in the past. In fact, a growing number of practices are experimenting with some highly untraditional but frequently effective arrangements, as discussed in the box on page 17. Relative job security, professional satisfaction and the opportunity to practice in an environment of respect compensate for not crossing the threshold to becoming co-owners.

## New Partner Arrangements

When you find an associate who is partner material, move on to the next important issue: Specific arrangements with your freshly-minted partner. Although deals vary widely, based on personalities, projected economics, specialty and more, focus on some basic details as a starting point. Be sure to consider the five issues detailed below.

These points, first discussed years ago, continue to make sense for most private groups despite managed care's growth. Though by no means automatically appropriate for every practice, you need to consider and decide on each. Then periodically review them; your practice and the health care environment change rapidly and often.

▸ *Stock purchase.* The new member buys enough stock to become an equal shareholder. Base the price on the practice's modified net book value. That way,

> **Consider 'Part-time' Partner Arrangements**
>
> In the past few decades, experts have identified a growing tension between "Baby Boom" generations doctors and their younger counterparts. Author and professor Mitchell D. Kusy, PhD, says young doctors today show great reluctance — even refusal — to "sell their souls" to the practice.
>
> Recent graduates are more interested in quality of life issues. While they desire fewer work hours and more flexible schedules, many still express interest in a partnership track.
>
> Bullying your way through existing partners' insistence that new members work in the same high-paced style risks your ability to attract and keep qualified physicians, says psychologist John-Henry Pfifferling, PhD, who specializes in helping physicians recognize and cope with stress.
>
> Face up to this tough issue. Appoint a small task force to develop a partner policy that's sensitive to new and existing partner needs without compromising your overall group vision. But be sure the resulting policy addresses your core values and non-negotiable partner obligations.

the price does not reflect either accounts receivable or goodwill value.

If the new partner cannot comfortably pay the figure in a lump sum, permit payment in installments with interest. You can offer different classes of stocks, depending on how equal you want new associates to be from the get-go.

- ▸ *Income discounts.* The new member shares in the group's income division format, but at less-than-full income shares. In each of the first four years, multiply his/her share by an increasing percentage (60% the first year, 70% the second, and so on, until achieving full parity in year five).

Termed an "inexact buy-in," such an approach more or less recognizes accounts receivable and practice goodwill. Or you could make it an "exact buy-in," discounting the full income shares over a number of years to "buy into" a specifically-calculated dollar sum based on a precise computation of the practice's accounts receivable and goodwill value.

- *Separation arrangements.* If the newer member dies or leaves the practice for any reason, be sure you can repurchase his/her stock using the same formula described above.

Beyond that, while a senior member may be entitled to a considerable pay-out or separation pay (recognizing a full interest in accounts receivable and goodwill value, as the members prospectively agree on these factors), the young member's right to separation pay phases up over as many as 10 years. For example, the junior would receive no separation pay if s/he quit or died during the first co-ownership year, 10% if the departure were in the second year, and so on.

- *Vacation time and sick pay.* Rather than equal entitlement right off the bat, phase up these features during a new member's early years as a co-owner.

- *Restrictive covenant.* If legal in your state, these days an associate should be bound by restrictive covenants. Continue that restriction into partnership status, but make it consistent with that of the other partners. We prefer a perpetual restriction, though sometimes it lapses after perhaps a decade of practice.

In addition, if you are a solo physician, consider making the new member's status subject to a stock option that allows the group to repurchase his/her shares and terminate the employment if you no longer wish to practice together. This right may be perpetual, though negotiations often result in limiting it to perhaps 10 years.

## The 'inexact' buy-in

Managed care still produces uncertainty about practice goodwill values and buy-ins. With goodwill values moderating, many young doctors wonder whether buy-ins should be less expensive than in the past. Senior members, though, are reluctant to bring in another full partner under bargain-basement terms.

In the face of such uncertainty and potential for dispute, we cautiously opt for the inexact buy-in method. The exact method is less likely to produce results fair to all members, and no better alternatives yet exist.

Here's how various health care consultants and attorneys size up the challenge:

■ *Inexact buy-ins make the most sense*
   *Consultant Michael J. Parshall*

   "With such uncertainty in the near future, and since virtually all buy-ins occur over a period of years, any arrangement setting an exact goodwill value is subject to huge debate. It is at risk of becoming outdated by rapid change in the market before the buy-in period ends. Inexact buy-ins make more sense than ever.

   "While the traditional inexact buy-in works by gradually increasing the junior partner's income share, I foresee another approach: The senior members may start insisting on a guaranteed 'first draw on income' for themselves before the newer partner's share can step up to full parity."

   This approach makes sense so long as the young partner has minimum income assurances, but it also depends on where the bargaining clout lies in negotiating new-doctor contracts.

■ *Ownership carries rewards and risks*
   *Consultant Paul W. Smith, CPBC*

   "I suspect that we'll likely see more small buy-ins, since the income pools may shrink. Structuring the buy-in on an inexact method makes it self-adjusting to the changing environment. If income decreases after becoming a partner, that's a risk the new doctor must be willing to take to become partner. After all, ownership carries both rewards and risks.

   "Some practices make less money because they don't work smarter, with less effective management and less ability to react. In these instances, it's only fair that the younger doctor pay less and the senior doctors receive less as a result of these inefficiencies."

We've favored the inexact buy-in method for years; confusion over goodwill value makes it more compelling.

■ **Percentages depend on practice economics**
*Attorney and consultant Robert A. Wade*

"I don't see a better alternative for new co-owners than the inexact approach. It need not always be on the oft-cited 60%-70%-80%-90% model. The percentages should depend on an individual practice's economics.

"But any increasing share of income entitlements gives the greatest flexibility while giving both sides some sense of concreteness — namely that there is a deal."

■ **Promise some income progression**
*Attorney and consultant Geoffrey T. Anders*

Anders anticipates that uncertainty about goodwill values will lead many more groups to make no income sharing promises at all. For instance, a senior doctor or group might simply say that due to medicine's economy, they can't promise anything beyond assuring full parity by a certain date:

"I don't see how the 'no promises' approach will sell in the near term, for young doctors won't accept it. In not too many years, though, I expect that all physicians will be paid on a salaried basis not related to any specific income progression or promises of parity at all."

So our generally-favored inexact buy-in method overwhelmingly makes the most sense these days. You can offer a young doctor an arrangement not hung up on goodwill value which — though still recognized as a factor in many (but by no means all) private practices — is more speculative now than ever before.

Do the math to see if the standard 60%-70%-80%-90% progression fits your economics. Recognize, though, that some percentage progression may remain your best approach.

## Decouple the Buy-in Arrangements

While deals vary widely, early-year income reductions and stock purchase will likely be part of your buy-in arrangement with new partners. We suggest decoupling these two main parts of your agreement.

Doing so helps insulate against the IRS possibly claiming that taking less pay as part of a buy-in deal is really a disguised part of the stock purchase. Conversely, it rebuts an IRS argument that the group cannot tax-deduct the "separation pay" upon a retiring member's departure, because the payments are instead part of buying back the stock. Decoupling also makes sense because you should have different reasons and criteria for becoming a co-owner than for sharing in a member's compensation pool.

### The two-step process

Healthcare consultant and attorney Daniel M. Bernick recommends and routinely implements for his clients a traditional six-month time differential between the start of income sharing and stock co-ownership. Offer stock ownership to recognize certain factors like:

- ✓ Attaining board certification

- ✓ Satisfying the Board of Directors (the other partners) about the physician's reliability as a co-owner to be trusted in the practice's business management

- ✓ Helping make the practice grow more profitable by various work and/or business attributes

### Different income-sharing criteria

On the other hand, perhaps a young doctor should not yet become a co-owner but should still share in group income for reasons unrelated to those for stock purchase, such as:

✓ Having completed satisfactory employment for a stated time period, thus deserving pay higher than that of just an associate

✓ Achieving an agreed-to productivity level

✓ Satisfying the board that s/he merits "senior" status based on factors like developing new referral patterns, taking on important clinical responsibilities, etc.

Put the arrangements in different contracts, suggests Bernick. When the buy-in time approaches, put the stock purchase terms into one document and the income sharing arrangements into another. They actually belong separately anyway — in the Shareholders' Agreement and the Employment Agreement, respectively (assuming a professional corporation or limited-liability corporation or partnership [*LLC/LLP*]).

## The IRS factor

Back in the early 90s, a new tax provision alerted medical practice advisors to a possible IRS attack on new member buy-ins to co-ownership. That law (Code section 1060) required reporting any change in ownership involving at least a 10% interest. Unless practicing with 11 or more partners, bringing in a new partner or buying out a retiring, deceased or withdrawing partner became a reportable event.

Section 1060 didn't change the law, but having to report a buy-in's details opens your new partner's deal to closer review. It could lead the IRS to treat his/her typical first few years of income reductions as disguised parts of a capital purchase, thus changing the intended tax treatment. Perhaps worse, it could lead the IRS to determine that a senior member's buy-out doesn't deserve the tax treatment that is extremely important to the ongoing group.

To avoid the problem of the buy-in, the advice goes, just separate the date when the young doctor purchases stock in the practice corporation from the date s/he starts receiving reduced shares of group income. Then report under section 1060 the stock purchase on its own terms without reporting the income reduction.

You could similarly provide for a two-part pay-out structure, perhaps requiring a senior to sell back stock upon reaching a stated age (perhaps 62 or 65) but not starting the income pay-out (usually called "separation pay" or "deferred compensation") until s/he actually retires.

### Owner versus worker status

Besides, decoupling stock purchase from income sharing furthers the philosophy differentiating between being a good physician and being a good partner. Ownership should be based at least partly on certain entrepreneurial skills, not just on treating patients.

It is more difficult to separate the capital (stock) and income (compensation) elements in a pay-out when a partner retires. Still, having a member resell his/her stock upon reaching, say, age 65 (whether or not the doctor retires at that age) has some logic. The senior physician thus — at least technically — leaves major decisions up to the younger partners who will be affected by them for years to come. In doing so, s/he strengthens the argument that later separation pay (starting upon actual retirement) has no relation to capital values.

## Computing the Stock Purchase Price on Net Book Value

The stock purchase segment of the buy-in is fortunately less muddy, but presents its own unique wrinkles. We subscribe to the "net book value" approach because it relates to a practice's *capital* aspect (as opposed to the accounts receivable and goodwill value). And usually the resulting stock price is low enough that co-ownership is affordable.

Beware, however, that this approach can unintentionally make you a generous seller.

The balance sheet likely dictates what your new partner must pay to become a shareholder. Its net book value figure takes into account your equipment's and furnishing's original cost, as reduced by depreciation. It also includes cash on hand, corporate investments and deposits, less bank loans and other liabilities.

### Overlooked assets

However, reliance on accounting reports may leave valuable assets off the books. These items are often tremendously useful in the office, and sometimes worth quite a lot. But unless you catch the accounting exclusion, a new partner's stock purchase price may not reflect them. The following four items are most often overlooked during new partner buy-ins:

- *Leased equipment.* Some practices lease larger items like x-ray equipment, paying rent plus interest for a number of years and then buying them at a minimal price. The balance sheet will not list such equipment as an asset, nor does the rental obligation show as a liability. It may, though, have significant book and actual value had the practice bought it.

- *Section 179 assets.* Under current tax law you may choose to immediately write off in the range of $20,000 of equipment and furniture bought each year. Since the items were never treated as purchased assets subject to depreciation, they may also be missing from your balance sheet despite their usefulness and value to the practice.

- *Insurance prepayments.* Suppose you pay a large annual malpractice insurance premium in late December. If your practice's fiscal year ends December 31, the net book value is reduced even though the payment really applies to the next year. Logic calls for adding the prepayment back to your corporate balance sheet.

- *Supplies and inventory.* Most medical practices do not have enough cash invested in medical supplies to count toward the buy-in price. Yet some groups maintain substantial inventories; for instance, ophthalmologists frequently carry contact lenses and spectacles, oncologists stock chemotherapy drugs and family physicians keep medications on hand to dispense to patients.

# Structuring the Buy-In for a High Value Practice

While our described arrangements work well for most small to mid-sized groups, they may not work for highly-valued practices — mainly because the new member cannot afford them.

This is often the case for practices with substantial and expensive amounts of equipment on hand or which continue to produce unusually generous incomes. Sometimes associates expecting to buy into these valuable groups cannot yet produce enough income to support the expensive buy-in.

The problem may be compounded if the group paid a very high salary to attract the young doctor in the first place. Along with a generous incentive bonus, a high starting salary makes it nearly impossible to structure an income give-up that will not severely cut into take-home pay. It seems logical that the associate will still have plenty of income to live on. Nevertheless, to the young doctor, it's a pay cut.

## Watch the stock purchase portion

Furthermore, the stock-purchase price based on expensive equipment values may be quite high even if paid over a number of years. These payments typically come from after-tax dollars and include a reasonable interest rate.

Some senior physicians even give equal stock ownership to younger doctors for free — an illogical approach, we think. Seniors may later be stung when their younger partners refuse to sell the stock back on the same terms.

All in all, the combination makes it hard to handle stock payments without suffering a decline in take-home pay. One solution: *Simply reduce or eliminate the buy-in.*

## Base buy-in on production

As a better solution, consider making the buy-in process depend on the associate's achieving a pre-set level of production compared to other partners. For instance, the buy-in might not begin until the young doctor's productivity level reaches 80% of all senior members' average production. In a two-doctor practice, the newer member must produce 40% of the group's receipts for the buy-in to commence. In a four-physician group, the starting point is 20%.

Attorney Bernick prefers this approach because the new member does not take an income hit until s/he is presumably able to afford paying fair value. It also sends an appropriate signal to the young physician: *Pull your own weight in terms of revenue production.*

The obvious flaw in this approach: Managed care pressures groups to de-emphasize traditional production in favor of practice efficiency. Still, most small to mid-size groups continue to reward members on individual productivity. Thus, apply the same system to new partner buy-ins in order to maintain consistency.

Some practices make it nearly impossible for a new associate to produce like the seniors. For example, a new surgeon may handle most of the in-office medical work while surgeries go to the senior partner. Or the new internist sees more capitated patients while the seniors handle full-fee visits.

## Consider attractive salary progression to attract new associates

As you adapt your compensation formula to changes in managed care, apply Bernick's approach to your formula — especially where capitation formulas (still emphasizing work performance) remain a factor. For instance, a group in transition can combine a minimum production requirement with a minimum efficiency rating or similar managed care standard.

This system provides for an automatic buy-in when the associate's production hits the target. Yet it need not mean that the senior partners automatically sell shares in the corporation and thereby give up control. You may limit the automatic mechanism so it only makes an associate eligible to share group income and accrue rights to a pay-out upon retirement, death or other departure — not to becoming a co-owner. (As previously discussed, do not sell an ownership interest unless the young doctor's entrepreneurial and management capabilities warrant doing so.)

In any event, you may be able to hold a good young physician even without offering partner status right on schedule. In this new century, opportunities in some specialties are fewer, and an attractive salary progression — albeit not as attractive as a full partner's share in your practice — will hopefully still hold vast appeal.

# Special Situations in New Partner Buy-ins

Beyond the buy-in basics, be alert to some significant special considerations — wrinkles in the usual set-up that may become extremely important if you don't face them up front. To end this chapter, we present these key situations.

- *Senior partner's rights.* A solo practitioner taking on a first partner may rightfully be concerned about losing control over practice decisions when the new member (we'll call her "Junior") comes into equal ownership. And yet, to make her a less-than-equal partner flies against the concept of professionals equally involved in a joint enterprise; Junior will probably refuse such lesser status. The problem becomes even worse if Dr. Senior takes on a second young partner, for then he could clearly be outvoted — or even voted out!

Dr. Senior can best serve his proper interests by reserving what we call "senior partner's rights" in the buy-in documents. These take the form of an option letting him at any time repurchase Junior's stock at the agreed pricing formula. Thus the two doctors can work as 50-50 "partners" — sharing in decisions as professional equals — while the senior member is protected in case they encounter a split-up situation. If it comes to that, Junior must leave and the practice stays with Dr. Senior.

While Bernick prefers handling the senior partner situation this way, he warns that even it may not deserve to go on forever. Somewhere along the line, Junior has probably earned the same protection as her senior partner. So consider calling for the option to expire when the buy-in period ends (typically four years).

- *Semi-personal assets.* It's fine to have Junior pay for her stock in the practice according to the balance sheet's recital of equipment, cash on hand and other productive assets. But small corporations often hold "semi-personal assets" like partners' cars, personal computers used by their families at home and perhaps even art collections.

Though corporate-owned, the partners consider them personal to themselves. Should the new member pay a price based on those values as well? After all, they're on the corporate balance sheet.

The simplest approach — having the seniors remove these special items from their corporation — involves adverse tax consequences they'll want to avoid. Instead, calculate Junior's buy-in stock price without including those assets and also carve that portion out of what she would receive if she later sells out. Provide in the seniors' documents for a correspondingly higher price and include distribution of their special assets to satisfy the extra price.

- *Sick pay, vacation and meetings.* Should a new partner be entitled to the same allowances as a senior member? It's not unusual for group documents to phase up vacation, sick pay and professional meeting absence, starting only slightly more generously than for an associate.

  For vacation time, you might give a first-year partner four weeks of paid absence if she was entitled to three in her last employee year; then perhaps five weeks a year in her next few co-owner years, and thereafter six weeks or whatever the regular partners get. Apply the same concept to meetings and sick pay allowances, phasing up to equal rights over three to five years as a member.

- *Sell-out protection.* What if you bring Junior into equal co-ownership and soon thereafter you sell the practice for a hefty sum? As an equal owner, Junior would share in that apparent bonanza despite short tenure (compared to seniors who served many years). We urge inserting special provisions phasing up a young member's share of any such buy-out price.

# Chapter 3

*Physician Leadership*

## The Critical Success Factor

Nearly all medical group practices fit one of three distinct governance models: the *fraternal* organization, the *basic business* organization and the *mature business* organization. Successful groups work to develop into mature business organizations, though they often continue to show attributes of all three models.

### Developing groups

A group in the first stage — the fraternal organization — consists of independent members voting to further their personal interests. Objectives are self-satisfaction, immediate gratification and personal security.

A fraternal organization member has little or no perception of a business entity capable of furthering its members' collective objectives. Instead, each individual's objectives come first. One vocal associate can shoot down ideas and plans — even those that obviously make sense. Hampered by veto style voting, these "marriages of convenience" move forward at glacial speed, if at all.

Even today, many small and mid-sized groups act like fraternal organizations, with little common vision and no stated mission. What management exists merely serves the administrative needs of the individual doctors.

Medical groups are often slow to move beyond the fraternal stage. Neither doctors' training nor their networking with colleagues (e.g., the medical staff) provides other experience or role models. Since the fraternal organization does little to foster trust or shared vision, physicians feel little motivation for change. Many groups resist abandoning the "every-doctor-is-an-island" format until the practice grows so complicated, with decision-making so burdensome, that the group's continued existence is threatened.

## The second stage

Upon reaching six or more physicians, a group practice often achieves a certain level of operational interdependence. Sometimes (like when the group makes a significant investment in a physical plant) the need for more sophisticated governance structures becomes apparent. In this next stage of development — the basic business organization — executive function tends to concentrate in one or a few physicians. And management comes to mean more than making sure bills are paid and receivables collected.

At this stage, management serves to develop and implement policies benefiting the group over and above individual members' interests. As the doctors begin to see themselves as members of a greater whole, they become willing to develop longer-term plans and sometimes even defer current income for reinvestment in the practice. Many group members even begin to share a common vision and mission.

As group interests slowly overtake individual interests, a basic business organization begins to outgrow its previous "decision paralysis" caused by blackball voting. It arrives at decisions through consensus rather than through unanimity.

## Achieving maturity

A growing sense of interdependence also fosters greater trust among the partners. This in turn permits further development into the third model, a mature business organization. Here a small Board of Directors recognizes its fiduciary responsibility to the owner-shareholders. The group elects Board members on their merits as leaders and executives, rather than as representatives of a particular generation or specialty training.

Managing physicians function with clear reporting lines. Leaders identify and groom apparent heirs to the physician leadership before they have to accept full responsibility. With a deliberate succession plan, the group avoids operational breakdowns and loss of direction.

## Addressing Business Planning

Few groups fully achieve this last stage of development. Although the need is clear, most lag behind. To compete against and contract with large, well-capitalized and strongly-led business organizations now dominating many medical practice markets, physician groups must develop in a like style. And to work in partnership with payors and integrated systems, practices must develop similarly-structured organizations.

We are, though, beginning to see surprising glimmers of practices moving into this more mature phase. A few forward-thinking groups are seriously addressing business planning concerns and recognizing the need for a sophisticated compensation approach that rewards physicians in their multiple roles.

In many cases, physicians are finally beginning to recognize that their individual partner is not a competitor. Instead, they realize that hospital administrators, insurance executives and business entrepreneurs often pose greater threats as they champion *their* own organizational objectives.

A medical practice group's destiny rests in the hands of its owners. Developing into a mature, successful organization won't happen by chance. Work hard to engage every group member in developing a group vision, an organizational mission, and a workable strategy to realize both. Invest plenty of time and effort in strategic planning.

### Establishing direction

Medical group partners often admit that they don't really take enough time to make important decisions for their practices' future. Many groups attempt to schedule monthly business meetings, but fail to actually hold many sessions because of the routine pressures on their members. Other groups stick to their meeting schedules, but the sessions are too short to permit real accomplishment.

We've consistently recommended that partners schedule an extended meeting for undisturbed discussion of major issues facing the group. These meetings, which we call retreats, can range anywhere from a long half-day (perhaps 8:00 a.m. to 2:00 p.m.) to an entire weekend.

Retreats offer a variety of benefits. Holding them away from your office — perhaps even out of town — removes the usual distractions when partners attempt to deal with sensitive issues. Here's how to ensure the success of your group practice retreat:

- ■ *Appoint a planning chairman.* Someone must carefully plan the retreat, prepare its budget, establish specific goals and plan the agenda. Assign basic organizational responsibility to one of your physician-members. If your group has 10 or more partners, appoint a three-member committee. Certainly your manager or administrator can handle many of the details, yet there are enough sensitive matters in a successful retreat to make partner-level direction essential.

- ■ *Make attendance mandatory.* Physicians often find it "impossible" to achieve 100% attendance because one or more must cover the practice. Don't let this happen! Arrange for coverage by non-partner associates, respected hospital colleagues or even a locum.

- ■ *Prepare an agenda.* Your members deserve the opportunity to prepare their own thoughts for important discussion. Develop targeted topics, assign presentations and allocate specific time. Prepare the agenda in advance and distribute it to each partner as much as two weeks before the event. Make sure one unanimously-respected partner wraps up by summarizing the event's achievements.

- ■ *Appoint a facilitator.* S/he must lead the group discussion to a definite resolution without pressing for any personally-preferred decisions. While you can select your own administrator or one of the partners, perhaps the best choice is to hire an independent consultant who will be sensitive to the inter-partner chemistry and hidden agendas usually present in professional practices.

# Developing Leadership in Your Group

Pure democracy is pure rabble. When a practice does little more than take each day as it comes, there will come a day when there's no practice.

Truisms? Undoubtedly. But true nevertheless. If we re-clothe these two clichés in today's preferred language, we arrive at the founding principle of effective medical practice governance: *Your practice needs a managing doctor to envision the future, set goals, and position the practice for continued success.*

Basic management theory calls for having a single strong leader. Almost every type of organization — governmental, charitable, educational, commercial and even professional — thrives according to the quality of its chief executive officer (CEO). This principle applies to medical group practices, even though we still find some physicians who resist it.

Simply put, a medical group's success or failure *as an organization* depends primarily on its physician leadership.

## Major responsibilities

Some practices call the managing doctor a physician-leader, president or CEO, but exact title is not as critical as the ability to lead. In addition to envisioning the future, setting goals and positioning the practice for continued success, health care consultant Dorothy R. Sweeney says your CEO must also:

- *Serve as Chairman of the Board of Directors.* Oversee all business meetings, prepare an agenda for each meeting and make sure the group implements the decisions made.

- *Ensure that doctors conform to practice rules and procedures.* This authority covers infractions like physician lateness, inappropriate charting, inattention to details or any other disregard of specified practice rules.

- *Handle physician evaluations.* That means for both employed doctors and shareholders.

- *Work closely with the administrator.* That includes assigning tasks and seeing that those responsibilities are properly handled. The administrator should report directly to the CEO.

- *Create the practice's business plan.* With, of course, the guidance and backing of the Board of Directors and the administrator's assistance.

- *Position the practice appropriately.* Make sure the group is allied with the right health plans, maintains good (and mutually beneficial) relationships with hospital administrations, and positions itself with industry, physician groups and other health care alliances, along with investigating other non-traditional business opportunities.

- *Oversee all contracting.* That encompasses managed care, financing, joint ventures, employment and outsourced professional services.

- *Lead the advisory team.* Including administrators, supervisors and other physicians, the team oversees finances, business and clinical operations, information systems and personnel.

Healthcare attorney Daniel M. Bernick recommends creating a written job description for your group leader. It lets the managing partner know the group's expectations while providing an objective standard for individual group members to see what they get for their money.

**Just one, please**

When we say that every virtually every group needs one managing doctor, we really mean *just one*. Over the years we've seen fully democratic groups flounder, paralyzed by indecision, or worse yet, poisoned by dissension. Having just one doctor at the helm prevents confusion and duplication of effort, thus reducing costs and increasing morale.

Generally, the practice's governing body (which may be made up of the shareholders, a Board of Directors or an executive committee) elects its president for a set term of perhaps two to three years. It may reelect an incumbent. While president-for-life is not a winning idea, neither is serial rotation to give everyone a turn.

## Serving as visionary

Essentially, the managing doctor is the practice's visionary. S/he must recognize and cultivate allies, and assess and respond to competitors. In addition, s/he needs to step back and take a strategic view of the practice in order to predict future economic or social trends, develop new strategies and identify new technologies.

Having a vision is not enough. The managing doctor must be able to persuasively communicate this vision to other members of the practice. Such shared vision generates optimism and enthusiasm about adjusting to changed times and forging ahead.

## Acquired skills

Are *you* a candidate to be your practice's managing doctor? If not you, then who?

Of course, not everyone is suited for the position. Perhaps you — or someone you've tried to challenge — shied away from leadership roles thinking, "It's not for me. I'm not a natural leader." Well, it's time to divest yourself of that myth.

According to a remarkably useful book, *Leadership for Dummies,* authors Marshall Loeb and Stephen Kindel effectively debunk several myths about leadership, including the one about natural-born leaders.[1] You can acquire and sharpen all the skills you need to become an effective leader. The quality you require most is the "emotional intelligence"[2] to *embrace responsibility*.

Sometimes leaders accept responsibility thrust upon them — and they may do an adequate job. But the memorable leader — one who inspires people to go beyond what they think they're capable of — *embraces* responsibility. Unafraid of accountability, s/he says, "I *want* to do that!"

True leaders exhibit the following charactcristics. The real trick is being able to deliver these abilities with remarkable consistency:

✓ eliciting others' cooperation

✓ listening well

✓ placing other (organizational) needs above their own

---

[1] Published in 1999 by IDG Books Worldwide, Inc. (*www.idgbooks.com*); available in paperback or audiotape for less than $20 at almost any major bookstore.

[2] As described in Daniel Goleman's popular book, *Emotional Intelligence* (New York: Bantam Books, 1995).

## It's Not a Kingship

Being managing doctor is not the same as having total control of the practice, though. Rather, the leader is an important link in the chain of command, a liaison between the practice's owners and its administrator. In effect, the managing doctor runs interference for the owners, knowing when to make decisions to keep things moving without formally involving other partners. Just as importantly, s/he recognizes when problems warrant all partners' attention.

The managing doctor must also be ready to delegate, so be wary of appointing hands-on individuals. When a managing doctor sees that something needs to be done, s/he typically assigns the task to someone else in the practice, ensures that the assigned task is completed and reports back.

Another key aspect: handling non-clinical issues like negotiating managed care contracts, installing a management information system and assessing whether to initiate or join new strategic alliances.

### Identifying aptitude

Many doctors just aren't interested in such matters and, thus, are unlikely candidates for physician leadership. For some, the lack of interest results from having focused on other priorities in college, medical school and training. For others, the lack of interest in leadership is more deeply ingrained.

Given motivation to learn plus adequate training, however, potential physician-leaders become intellectually engaged, business-oriented and forward-thinking. Here's a quick test of your natural level of interest:

> Do you regularly read periodicals like *Barrons* and *The Wall Street Journal*? Or do you browse the Internet to keep up with general business developments? And do you enjoy sharing those interests with others?

Individuals with real interest and aptitude don't necessarily need an MBA to be an effective CEO, although some find pursuing such a degree worthwhile. If you're interested in higher-level business training, see our box on the next page.

## Business Training for Physicians

If you believe you have the right stuff to lead a group, you may want to sharpen skills and improve your performance as a managing doctor with top-quality education and training. Here are three good sources:

• **Graduate degree programs.** An increasing number of doctors are enrolling in excellent business schools with degree programs tailored expressly for physicians. A few examples: the Wharton School (University of Pennsylvania), the University of Wisconsin, Duke University, Northwestern University, the University of Arizona (at Scottsdale) and St. Thomas University.

• **American College of Physician Executives.** The ACPE, with status as an AMA-approved specialty society, is composed of MDs who devote all or part of their time to managerial responsibilities. While many of its members are employed fulltime by hospitals, health systems and managed-care organizations, many are private practice leaders, too. ACPE activities include a certification program and excellent educational programs. Contact ACPE at (800) 562-8088 or online at *www.acpe.org.*

• **Medical Group Management Association and The American College of Group Practice Executives.** The MGMA historically served only non-physician administrators, but in recent years a growing number of physicians have joined to take advantage of its skills and sophistication as well.

We consider its annual and regional section meetings among the very best sources of physician-level education. One of its assemblies, the Society for Physicians in Administration, is designed especially for doctors heavily involved in group practice leadership.

MGMA's education arm, the American College of Group Practice Executives provides a certification track to guide those seeking thorough executive training. Contact MGMA at (877) 275-6462 or on the Web at *www.mgma.com.*

**Evaluating peers**

Business acumen alone is not enough. Managing doctors must roll up their sleeves from time to time and do some dirty work. For example, CEO duties include evaluating the group's physicians and practice administrator, encouraging group consensus and resolving disputes. For many, it's particularly hard to evaluate a partner whose review is less than glowing.

If you're not willing to take charge during these difficult processes, don't even consider serving as your group's primary leader. And if you're unwilling to support — and submit to — your physician-leader's authority, you may not even belong in a group practice.

# Enable Your Managing Physician to Perform

Now that you understand the importance of physician leadership, you're ready to plug the right candidate into the job and move on, right? Not so fast!

How is the managing doctor going to find the time to perform? Often the doctor who should assume the task is so busy with patient responsibilities that s/he has little time to do much else.

One solution: Reduce the managing doctor's practice obligations by as much as one-half to free up the time needed for executive duties. Some practices pass the managing doctor's patients on to associate physicians, whereas others allow the CEO to devote one day a week to group leadership concerns.

**How the experts see it**

What do the nation's top medical consultants observe, and what do they recommend to their clients?

L. Michael Fleischman continues to see smaller groups totally eschew the leadership position. Still, a number of his clients are beginning to identify the need for a managing partner or CEO. He tells such practices that a doctor will have to reduce clinical time from 10% to 25%, roughly an afternoon or two per week, to handle executive/administrative duties.

Fleischman recommends flat compensation, at least $12,000 per year above normal income share or a small percentage of practice revenue (but not more than 5%). If the CEO is performing duties properly, there will be no reduction in the other partners' salaries; in fact, his/her work will spur an increase in everyone's income.

Other advisors agree on the time-off issue. For example, consultant Gray Tuttle cites one group that divides all profits equally, thus allowing the CEO to reduce clinical time without taking a cut in pay.

Dorothy R. Sweeney says groups just installing a managing doctor typically wind up allowing the equivalent of a day per week (usually two clinical sessions) out of the practice schedule — but, she notes, very seldom is more time allowed, even where absolutely needed. After a while, as the value of physician leadership becomes more apparent, the partners may agree that their CEO needs and deserves more time away from office hours.

Vasilios J. (Bill) Kalogredis also notes that small groups often are reluctant to give any time off for fear of lost revenue. But forward-thinking practices acknowledge the importance of leadership by providing a 20% to 25% caseload reduction equaling about one day per week.

### Another approach

Kalogredis and several other consultants report that some of their clients take another approach. These groups excuse their managing partners from weekday call responsibilities, perhaps on the reasoning that the CEO's time demands impose a different intrusion on personal and family life. None of the consultants, though, see groups excusing their leaders from weekend call.

Bette Warn says smaller practices that are gun-shy about giving adequate clinical time off should hire a higher-level manager to help make up the difference. Such a person provides the administration, strategic management and business development desired of the CEO without losing the income a top-quality partner produces for the practice.

But even the best "lay" administrators seldom — if *ever* — carry the kind of authority and respect among a group of physicians. Of course you need capable management, but your group won't reach its potential without leadership at the physician level.

James N. Ramsey also recognizes that need, but cautions that many groups are doomed from the start because of inter-partner biases about having one of their peers become a leader. That's where continuing education comes in. Smart groups give their CEO a special allowance for business leadership training, along with an extra week off for attending meetings and courses.

## Pay for Valuable Leadership

Finding time is only part of the puzzle. Even more challenging: fairly compensating the managing doctor, especially when members are paid on individual productivity. The list below details the most common methods for compensating a group practice CEO. And the box on page 42 provides our recommendations to help you think broadly about physician-leader compensation.

- ■ *Percentage of net income.* Paying your managing physician a percentage of the overall practice income (net revenue less expenses) often makes the most sense. Paying on this basis carries a built-in reward for making the practice more profitable. And group members tend to go along with this plan more easily, because they can see that they're "getting their money's worth."

- ■ *Flat stipend.* Setting a flat management fee, while a common approach, poses several difficulties. First, how do you determine a fair amount? We've seen management stipends for leaders in small to medium-size groups range anywhere from $1,000 to over $6,000 per month.

   Some groups arrive at a figure by asking the managing partner to take, for example, one day per week for administrative work. Then they pay a fee equivalent to 20% of his/her normal production.

   Note, however, two problems with this scheme:
   1. A flat fee provides no financial reward for good management. Whether your leader does a good or a poor job, the compensation remains the same.

> **Guidelines for Defining Physician-Leader Compensation**
>
> Our consultants generally feel a managing partner deserves at least enough pay to be made whole. That is, if s/he must give up productive time seeing patients, don't let the reduced production cause a cut in the leader's income. Here's what we recommend:
>
> - Set goals for the CEO to achieve, just as if s/he were a non-doctor manager.
>
> - Reduce clinical demands by one or two sessions per week.
>
> - Consider excusing from night (not weekend) call.
>
> - Ensure that his/her regular income share is made whole, and consider extra pay of $1,000 to $3,000 per month or a percentage of practice revenue.
>
> - Give an allowance for leadership/management education — perhaps $5,000 per year and an extra week off for meetings.
>
> - Determine special pay and goals as part of the annual expense budget, not as a partners' income sharing function.

2. A flat fee often sparks controversy when members wonder if they're getting a reasonable return on their investment.

- **"Gross-up" approach.** Some groups sharing profits on relative productivity compensate their leaders for lost clinical time by "grossing up" their normal production. If the managing partner uses one day per week to do administrative work, then the group agrees to pay a salary based on five-fourths (125%) of his/her base production.

If the leader actually produces $25,000 in monthly revenue, they would calculate pay as if s/he had actually produced 125% of that, or $31,250 (before expenses). This method avoids penalizing the doctor by letting him/her take enough time to manage and lead. While this plan may work well under the Hippocratic Oath ("do no harm"), it provides virtually no incentive to do a good job, and doesn't really recognize the managing physician's leadership skills.

## Setting CEO pay and bonus

There's seldom a bonus dollar figure for extra pay among small groups, because most partners simply do not understand the need for a managing doctor — and hence do not give the concept enough credence, notes Sweeney. She urges setting a leader's pay so s/he earns about the same as if seeing a full patient load.

Similarly, consultant David Shipman says many of his group clients do not separately pay their so-called leaders, especially because even reasonable compensation can appear unreasonable in the eyes of the other partners. Still, he describes times when the senior member may receive 5% of the revenue, ostensibly for leadership duties, for three to five years, as younger members grow into senior status. It may be called a form of buy-in to partnership, but it carries with it payment for CEO-type responsibilities, at least for a limited time.

Larger groups, though, seeing the importance, more often compensate on a combination of "making whole" plus a bonus arrangement based on specific goals — just like for higher-level administrators. In that regard, Thomas Martin says that at the six- or seven-doctor level, CEO pay may be in the range of $1,000 per month, with the monthly figure going up to $3,000 as the group gets larger and the job's importance increases still more. Your large group should consider even higher pay if the leader-doctor is capable, is doing the job well, and if the group relies on his/her skills.

## Put it in the budget

Perhaps most importantly, Gray Tuttle urges addressing the issue of CEO pay as part of your budget process, rather than as a matter of partners' income sharing. Recognize that compensating the physician-executive depends on the value of the services to the group — thus requiring you to jointly identify the role, its responsibilities and realistic time requirements.

You may not set the pay rate at the same level as for clinical work, but value it fairly. And address it each year when you prepare the annual budget.

Obviously, you have to find the plan that works best for you and your partners. But recognize that successful groups almost always have strong leadership, and properly rewarding a good leader encourages him/her to step out and lead with confidence.

# Chapter 4

*Group Governance*

## Working Toward the Good of the Group

Old folklore held that at least as many group practices broke up — over money, personal jealousies, or simple contrariness — as were put together, making for good chatter in the doctor's lounge when the latest local group implosion occurred. But, of course, the opposite was true: The number of group practices almost doubled in much of the 1990s, from around 8,000 to more than 15,000, and has increased still further after that count.

Such growth seems remarkable since groups are almost designed to self-destruct. Medical training reinforces perfectionism, individual achievement, compulsion and competitive behavior — not the recipe for a satisfying practice environment. Thus it is not surprising that most group practice organizations developed as fraternal entities.

Group expectations, outside of productivity, rarely get articulated, formalized or enforced. Anyone with a medical license making it past an initiation period of only a year or two is asked to join the club. Once a member, physicians freely behave as their personal idiosyncrasies or whims move them. Antisocial behavior rarely gets reined in.

This sometimes leads to extreme circumstances. For example, one group had no mechanism in place to fire a partner. When one of the members was rightly accused of sexual misconduct with patients, everyone else had to resign from the practice *en masse*.

### Evolution of group practice

Nevertheless, despite its shortcomings, group practice is clearly the option of choice. What started as largely a desire by solo physicians for call relief and ensured coverage for vacations has blossomed into multiple advantages. Doctors quickly latched onto the obvious economic advantage of sharing overhead.

That simple gain led them to recognize that, as a practice's patient base grows with multiple providers, it can support new technologies and subspecialties. The bottom line: clearly higher incomes for doctors in group practices.

These advantages of group practice in a fee-for-service environment translated well as managed care became virtually universal. Doctors recognized that larger entities could both manage risk and negotiate service contracts better than could soloists or very small groups. Indeed, some groups will likely evolve beyond their traditional specialty boundaries into disease management organizations focused on caring for the complete needs of individuals beset by certain conditions.

**Individual interests must take backseat to group success**

To make that metamorphosis most effective, though, the traditional group must mature beyond its members' me-first attitude. This maturity should evolve naturally, but the elements of individualism and competitiveness built into medical practice argue against it. Members must learn to curtail individual interests in favor of the group's greater interests.

All partners must submit with good grace to peer evaluation, confident that their reviewers have no agenda other than constructive suggestions to improve the group. Group members may require training in the social competencies and other crucial aspects of collaboration stunted by fierce intellectual effort of completing medical training. (See the accompanying box on the next page for more on the importance of emphasizing non-clinical attitudes in group practice.) Most importantly, all group members must learn a more supportive and nurturing approach to partner problems.

For instance, in the every-man-for-himself fraternal organization atmosphere, each member was expected to participate fully in the demands placed on the group. But mature groups reject this credo, opting instead to tailor some of the individual member's practice demands. Younger physicians often feed this need for change by insisting that there's more to life than practicing medicine.

**Structure the group to prevent burnout**

Traditionalists argue that physicians rise above these concerns — that medicine properly requires long hours, intense pressures and many frustrations. But these items also can lead to burnout.

# Require Non-Clinical Training for *All* Group Members

Along with urging that all group members serve the practice by assuming some non-clinical duties, Florida management consultant James M. Ramsey suggests going further. His idea makes great sense: "I recommend my clients require all shareholders to attend one or two days a year of continuing education in non-clinical areas. The practice would pay the out-of-pocket expense and the physician must take the time to attend without additional reimbursement. The courses may be in leadership (as most state medical societies offer), in healthcare socio-economic issues, or in practice management subjects approved by the group; they may be offered by your specialty or area medical society, by a professional seminar organization or perhaps by the MGMA or ACPE — so long as they meet group criteria for approval."

A group's collective knowledge is among the most important factors for its success. If some members have that knowledge and others either don't know or don't care, reaching consensus on critical issues becomes that much more difficult and contentious. And unless all members truly understand the importance of moving along, the gap between leadership and partner-members becomes almost too great to span. The consequences of such a gap are predictable, as Ramsey notes:

- Partners view the Board or Executive Committee as too autonomous
- The Board/Committee gets out of touch with its members
- Distrust sets in
- Out-of-Board meetings ('parking lot meetings') vicariously manage the group and undermine its leadership

Requiring every member to undergo non-clinical education is a fascinating idea; we agree that it can help make a group more effective. Too many practices are held back by a few members who don't understand present-day issues but unfairly influence decisions based on what they *don't* know. Bringing them into the 21st century on socio-economic concerns as well as clinical issues typically proves a worthwhile investment.

And burnout, in turn, has led to more than a few early retirements, leaving the group poorer for the loss of a senior member.

The group that believes everyone must contribute on all fronts fails to take advantage of the individual fortes — be they political talents, business acumen or leadership skills — of their members. At a time when competition for patients and payors is intensifying, groups cannot afford to lose what these members offer the practice.

### Balance personal and professional demands

Your practice likely spends time and money measuring patient satisfaction, but are group members as likely to give the same thought to measuring physicians' satisfaction?

As the subject rarely comes up in groups, it's important to make regular barometer checks, says physician well-being expert John-Henry Pfifferling, Ph.D. Unfortunately, many physician leaders have no idea that their doctors are unhappy, he notes. And that means these leaders don't recognize the importance of implementing some sort of method to measure provider satisfaction.

In his work with medical groups around the country, Pfifferling sees all sorts of stressors that put physicians at high-risk for burn-out and group departure. He emphasizes two current influences that compound the typical day-to-day stressors of scheduling: income concerns and clinical decision-making.

First, hospital administrators — themselves under terrible pressures — lack patience with physicians jockeying for services and positioning. That almost adversarial relationship adds to physician-leaders' stress levels. Pfifferling cites constituents battling for limited equipment funding as an example.

Second, practice pressures today breed a serious "brain drain," with more and more physicians looking to depart their practices. Pfifferling's worked with practices where the bulk of physicians have given their names to headhunters and nobody knows. While the physician-leaders meet and develop strategic plans for their practices, a large percentage of their doctors are more committed to looking elsewhere.

### Deal with these tough topics

Because physicians often avoid "touchy-feely" matters in partner interactions and avoid conflict at all costs, they're reluctant to address these issues head-on — but you must consider raising them for discussion if a well-being issue threatens to undermine your group.

The following list presents topics for conscientious *discussion*, not merely a checklist to be filed away. Wise groups whose members are willing to deal with physician/provider satisfaction are most likely to remain viable for the long haul. So consider scheduling a special meeting, or a full-practice retreat, to deal with these tough issues:

- Regularly assess practice goals and missions; where does the "balance" fit in?

- Regularly review the practice's organizational health.

- Privately give feedback when someone is overloaded.

- Schedule meetings so they don't interfere with family time.

- Hire a locum "house doctor" so you can hold meetings during work time.

- Offer skills workshops on balance, career development, mentoring and stress management.

- Establish quality assessment (QA) guidelines that do *not* reward workaholic behavior.

- Set up standards of interpersonal behavior so you can systematically change "imbalance."

- Establish a promotion policy that takes diverse workstyle or pace into consideration.

- Learn peers' professional exhausters so you can better allocate those exhausters.

- Establish a preventive "disruptive physician" policy.

# Governance Issues in Everyday Practice

Central to the success of any group practice is the realization that the practice is what counts. Individuals are certainly important, but never let one person's priorities outweigh what's best for the group. Two ways to ensure the practice comes first:

- ✓ Create the right kind of employment agreements/contracts.
- ✓ Evaluate the performance of all physicians regularly.

### Protect the group with employment agreements

Employment agreements must protect the interest of the group, says health care attorney Keith M. Korenchuk. Many doctors' employment contracts were drawn up in an era when group priorities and physician governance were relatively unimportant. Those days are clearly over; it's time to reevaluate old agreements. Look at these provisions:

- *Duties.* Specify how work is assigned and scheduled, the manner in which work is performed, and — for a newly employed physician — the chain of command.

- *Other activities.* Prohibit other medical practice except as permitted by the group.

- *Compensation.* Maintain flexibility so the group can modify members' compensation without having to amend the agreement.

- *Administrative and practice considerations.* Ensure that the group (not the physician) runs the business, hires personnel, owns the medical records, etc.

- *Quality of care.* Make clear that physicians must participate in programs that ensure the appropriateness of care and track outcomes.

- *Good citizenship.* Assert the right to evaluate intangible issues, such as cooperation and office demeanor as well as clinical performance, and to establish disciplinary authority for non-compliant or unprofessional conduct.

- *Term.* Have a fixed term without automatic renewal for new physicians. For established doctors, set a term (one year) with automatic renewal from year to year (but include a notice provision allowing the group to amend or terminate annually).

- *Termination.* Allow a short period (such as 30 days) to terminate employment at any time without reason. Provide immediate termination for breach of contract.

- *Effect of termination.* Specify what happens to accounts receivable, medical records, compensation and any subsequently-arising liabilities upon a member's departure.

- *Restrictive covenant.* Insist on a reasonable, enforceable restriction against competing with the group after departure. As Korenchuk puts it, you are better armed with a restrictive covenant than without it, whether or not you expect to assert it.

## Keep it simple

As you implement these concepts, keep in mind that the overriding purpose of partnership and corporate agreements is to help your members work together comfortably. For that reason, don't make contract provisions too complicated.

One practice we know of had partnership agreements that ran over 60 single-spaced pages. Members were totally confused by their contracts. Worse yet, partner and associate defections revealed the group's poor interpersonal climate — partly due to members' lack of confidence in their arrangements.

Some attorneys believe that only complicated arrangements can address complex concerns. That's somewhat true, but only up to a point. Overall, simplicity best serves your group's needs. Thus, if you get a contract that fails the tests of relative simplicity and layman's ability to understand, insist on another draft — or get another lawyer!

## Selling it

Even if your lawyer prepares the simplest of agreements, don't assume physicians — especially partners — will simply buy into it.

After all, how can you convince a partner to surrender his/her personal security by consenting to changes like those described above? The answer is simple logic. Security rides with *group* — above personal — success. Some sacrifice of individual rights becomes essential to accomplish the greater goal. If some members don't accept this point, you have to decide how to proceed. Perhaps you'll confront a marginally-valuable partner with a "sign it or leave the group" ultimatum. Or you may grandfather those partners who refuse, applying the new structure to new members.

## Develop a 'Best-of-Class' Attitude

Consider not only issues governing individuals in the group, but the overall attitude you possess. In her extensive work with practices around the country, healthcare attorney and consultant Sandra McGraw has taken note of the attitudes and attributes most common to highly successful groups. You can certainly improve your practice's — and individual physicians' — performance by keeping the following traits in the forefront.

***Open minds.*** Physicians in best-of-class practices show a willingness to entertain new ideas and concepts. So in general, they *(1) actively seek out advice.* Successful doctors often hire professional advisors they've come to trust. They value bringing in an objective expert who can help sort out random ideas and evaluate them to see if they make sense for the practice. Outside advisors bring a breadth of experience to the table. They've seen what has and hasn't worked in similar situations.

With this same mindset, top performers *(2) boldly try new approaches.* After careful evaluation and planning, successful groups move forward and execute the plan. Even if things go awry, they tend to avoid blaming the planner. Rather, they learn from their mistakes and move on.

***Accurate self-image.*** While open to new ideas, top physicians don't follow every new fad, because they *(3) know what they're good at* and focus their energy on exploiting that talent. A gifted specialist recognizes where s/he produces the most revenue and doesn't feel the need to do everything him- or herself. Members of the group complement, rather than threaten one another with different skill sets.

***Adaptive approaches.*** While not afraid of hard work, high earners *(4) learn how to maximize efficiency and productivity* by "working smarter." They sometimes work longer hours than average (usually without complaining), but they willingly modify their practice styles to get the most done in the least amount of time. However, these doctors have sharpened their communication skills to the point where patients don't feel rushed through the office.

***In control.*** Finally, practices that achieve outstanding performance usually *(5) understand and exploit all the ways they can generate revenue.* For example, ophthalmologists often control revenue-producing technologies and facilities like lasers and ambulatory surgery centers (ASCs). By running fully-equipped offices and operating (or controlling) ASCs, they fine-tune their operations to move patients and procedures through the practice with ease.

Attitudes and philosophies naturally defy measurement. But you can look at your group's "culture" to see if it demonstrates open thinking and a willingness to embrace change. As a group, spend some time away from the practice to sort through your vision, mission and strategic plan. Make or renew a commitment to excellent patient care and superior business practices. Remain true to your core values; then be willing to change anything else to achieve your vision.

# Evaluate Your Partners — and Yourself

Employment contracts prove relatively worthless if you don't take the time to evaluate how physicians perform under them. So set up a formal review process for all physicians in your group, including partners.

The old traditional stand, "No one has the right to tell me how to do my work," just doesn't cut it any more. A rising level of impatience among partners in good quality groups calls for more attention to performance. With medicine becoming so much more competitive — and less automatically successful — members realize that their own futures may be damaged by their partners' shortcomings. They can no longer afford to let a partner's weaknesses or failures go unchecked.

## Propose a routine

Propose to your partners a specific evaluation routine. Entrust responsibility for coordinating the program to the practice's managing doctor or another highly trusted partner. Ask that doctor, perhaps aided by your lay administrator, to draft an evaluation form. Use the sample on page 56 to guide you, but tailor it to meet the specific needs of your practice.

To get wary partners to buy into the concept, ask them to help tailor the evaluation program. (You need their input anyway.) Circulate a list of performance standards, asking each partner to prioritize their importance. Make sure the list covers all areas, including:

- ✓ *Clinical.* Handling difficult diagnostic problems
- ✓ *Interpersonal.* Dealing with referrers and difficult patients
- ✓ *Personal commitment.* Taking on late afternoon admissions or assuming committee assignments

Leave a few blank spaces for members to write in their own suggestions. Use the replies to draft a proposed evaluation form accommodating your partners' views and your own sense of important standards. Present the form and proposed program details at the next partner meeting. It's more apt to win approval because you asked for their input.

## Conducting the assessment

The next step is actually performing the evaluation. Start by distributing blank copies of your performance evaluation form to all partners. Ask them to evaluate other partners' strengths and weaknesses.

From there, the managing doctor schedules a private meeting with each member to review the evaluations and plan for the succeeding year's individual and group goals. Ask a member to do the same with the managing doctor (and remember to evaluate his/her leadership ability, as well).

Partner-level evaluations have a history of being useful the first time around and losing steam in succeeding years. Don't let this happen. Keep pressing to make sure constructive guidance is offered every year.

*Solving Partner-Level Challenges*

# Sample Physician Evaluation Form

**DATE:** _____  **PHYSICIAN NAME:** _____

Please evaluate on scale from 1-3 (3-outstanding; 2-satisfactory; 1-needs improvement*)
*Any score of 1 should have a note of explanation.

|  | SCORE: |  | SCORE: |
|---|---|---|---|
| **TECHNICAL PERFORMANCE:** | | | |
| Maintains a current knowledge of appropriate areas of specialty and medicine | _____ | Communicates knowledge of specialty effectively to referring physicians | _____ |
| Makes an effort to expand present knowledge base | _____ | | |
| **WORK HABITS:** | | | |
| Contributes willingly to group needs above the minimum expectation ("above and beyond the call of duty") | _____ | Adapts flexibly to changing daily practice demands | _____ |
| Shows positive attitude towards work | _____ | Establishes good rapport with patients, treats patients with respect | _____ |
| Can be relied upon to complete assignments and responsibilities eagerly, doing them well and promptly | _____ | Shows respect for supporting staff | _____ |
| Responds well to crisis, unexpected needs in group, etc. | _____ | Cultivates existing referral relations and gives good effort to develop new referral patterns | _____ |
| Functions well under pressure | _____ | Shows leadership in managing work environment and group matters | _____ |
| Keeps up with office/hospital charts and dictation | _____ | Keeps concerns about group finances in proper perspective | _____ |
| **NON-CLINICAL ASPECTS:** | | | |
| Teaches and leads supporting staff (both hospital and office) | _____ | Accepts responsibility in group corporate and business matters | _____ |
| Gives lectures, speaks to civic groups, etc. willingly | _____ | Accepts responsibility in hospital matters | _____ |
| Contributes to establishing and maintaining a good practice environment ("esprit de corps") | _____ | Supports professional and specialty society groups | _____ |

**OVERALL PERFORMANCE RATING:** (circle one)
Outstanding   Satisfactory   Needs improvement

**KEY STRENGTHS:** _____
_____

**OTHER COMMENTS:**
_____
_____
_____

**AREAS OF NEEDED IMPROVEMENT:**
_____
_____
_____

# Chapter 5

*Dealing with Problem Partners*

## Protect the Group Against Its Partners — Not Vice Versa

Even with good governance, you'll find yourself dealing with problem partners. Most physicians prefer to ignore behavior and performance problems, at least those that are non-clinical in nature, in the hopes that they'll go away on their own. Trouble is, they usually don't and you need mechanisms in place to deal with partners who have trouble getting along with staff, patients, hospitals and referrers and with other partners. The best start is to take a look at your partner agreements.

Imposing monetary penalties on a partner who fails to comply with coding requirements or otherwise causes difficulties for the group presents a knotty problem. Partners may not have the stomach to slap penalties or threaten termination, but it's important to at least have that *authority* before ever having to use it.

### Common stumbling blocks

Far too many groups run into a legal stumbling block as soon as they even consider sanctioning a member. The problems crop up in other ways too. Suppose, for instance, you need to change your compensation (income division) formula but one or a few members object. That's not unusual since any income division change likely benefits some members at the expense of others.

The stumbling block: Many groups' partnership agreements, bylaws, buy-sell or employment contracts lock in partners' rights. You may not legally be able to fire a member (even for egregious actions), change your compensation pattern or impose a penalty meant to "send a message" without unanimous or near-unanimous agreement.

Ensuring every co-owner an unalterable arrangement — after all, you're partners — may be the genteel, trusting way to go, but it's bad management. Professional firms of all sorts have learned that the onslaught of intense competition, lower revenues and changed priorities requires protecting the group against its partners, not the other way around!

## Review Your Partner Arrangements

So what can you do if your legal documents create "locked in" arrangements? Work toward changing them, says health care consultant and attorney Daniel M. Bernick. Better to get your house in order first, before really difficult problems crop up, than to let them slide and find yourself unable to deal with them when they actually arise.

The first step: Carefully review the controlling documents. Some corporate agreements call for amendment by majority or "supermajority" vote of all members, while many partner-level employment agreements have "rolling" one-year terms that the employer can revise. Others, unfortunately, can be amended only with all the original signers' consents.

While you'll want to review those documents yourself, be sure to have your attorney do so, too. Difficult contract law issues can easily crop up when you discuss underlying change, so you'll want to be prepared for them as you and your partners enter discussions.

### Keep matters 'impersonal'

Tell your partners that the power to amend is essential to protecting the group in the long run. Make clear that no one contemplates firing a partner, imposing sanctions, or even changing the compensation structure in this focus on revising your agreements. In the now-demanding "business" of healthcare, the successful group must be able to make changes if and when the need arises.

It may take strong but subtle leadership to convince partners that change is for the benefit of all — and to encourage them to continue the effort. If you have a specific but unspoken problem or partner in mind, you'll want to create the mechanism for dealing with it (or him/her) if things get worse. In that case, most of your partners may agree to proposed change while the silent target member (and his/her supporters) object fiercely. Keep the discussion focused on good group structure and avoid personalizing issues.

With your lawyer's guidance, move the group toward evaluating and then voting on specific document changes. If you get enough votes to approve the amendments, proceed to adopting and signing them.

## Dealing with resisters

But what about a partner who votes against and refuses to sign the new provisions? Unless they're adopted unanimously, Bernick suggests inserting a waiting period — as much as a year — before the new arrangements take effect. It's only fair to allow a partner to move on if fundamental changes in the agreement are contrary to his/her liking.

Perhaps s/he will come around during the waiting period and recognize that s/he would rather practice with the group despite the new deal. Or perhaps s/he will quit and sell out under the old agreement's terms. If you want a strong group, that's an acceptable risk you'll have to face now and then.

Try the same approach even if your documents require unanimous approval. The majority may insist on making the changes or else pulling out. Incredibly difficult problems can (indeed, typically *do*) arise when groups consider splitting, so be carefully guided by lawyers and consultants.

## An occasional impasse

Sometimes going to the brink just won't work. The legal documents may have locked things in so tightly that even the majority can't break them without losing control over issues like office location, practice name or even managed care contracts.

If this happens, partners will almost surely back off and hope the feared problems don't ever arise. That's not a good scenario but you'll have to live with it and hope. Effective physician leadership and experienced advice — along with good luck — will then have to suffice.

# Address Behavioral Handicaps

Evaluating partners means little if you have no intention of nipping problems in the bud. Clinical problems lend themselves to fairly rational discussions. Only the most defensive of partners will object to an even-handed assessment of how s/he can improve patient care. And groups impose penalties for mishandling documentation and coding because such errors can lead to disastrous Medicare fines and penalties. But when it comes to behavior issues and the evaluation uncovers long-ignored personality problems, you need expert advice on how to address them to protect your group.

One of the most common stresses of physician-leaders is the difficulty of dealing with an abusive, arrogant, technically superb but interpersonally-unskilled person, notes psychologist John-Henry Pfifferling. He warns that it's important to understand that social and behavioral handicaps frequently result in sub-par personal care that further fuels this physician's poor interpersonal relationships.

In other words, your cranky, temperamental, intolerant partner may be skimping on necessary sleep, exercise and relaxation. Or s/he may be overworking, overeating, or otherwise inappropriately trying to cope with stressors in the office or at home. Those behaviors often aggravate this person's inability to deal with others.

## Tolerating one member's bad behavior damages the group

Behaviorally-handicapped physicians mistreat patients, family members, peers and/or staff. The instances of mistreatment (whether alleged or perceived) eventually cause isolation by peers, revenge, sabotage and turnover of staff, loss of patients to the practice, and increased claims. Yet these same doctors may possess technically superb skills and shine as high-powered producers. This makes it even more important to deal with their problems in advance of crisis.

Such a doctor may simply have poor interpersonal skills, or s/he may be plagued by physical or emotional impairment problems. Some people feel safe venting home- and family-related stress in the workplace. And sometimes we simply run into a partner who seems to be a flat-out jerk! Whatever the reason, the behaviorally-handicapped doctor too easily gives rise to unhappy patients (prone to claiming malpractice), unhappy (and thus less-productive) staff and unhappy partners.

**Prescribe the four-step program**

As you receive reports about abrasive, hypercritical, caustic, hot-tempered, gruff, sexist, exhausted, burned-out, depressed, manic, or ultra-competitive peers, apply this four-step program for dealing with such behaviorally-handicapped — but typically unaware — physicians.

- ■ *Step 1: Definition.* Define reasonable and competent interpersonal behavior. Once you spell out your group's philosophy and approach to practice, you can audit actual performance and determine appropriate corrective interventions. (For the record, we recognize Dr. Pfifferling's point here, but fear that these principles are not easy to put in writing.)

- ■ *Step 2: Education.* Set up a mechanism for focusing on the interpersonal aspects of your practice. Education is an important part of it, so devote some of your CME budget to programs offering interpersonal skill training. It's important, too, for partners to confront the importance of behavior. Put it on the agenda of your partner meetings.

- ■ *Step 3: Evaluation.* Receive feedback on a regular basis. Don't let a member stray far off the acceptable course without some mechanism calling your attention to the problem. Patient satisfaction surveys are fine, but may not be enough. So try evaluating physicians every six months by circulating a questionnaire to randomly-selected patients. Look specifically for these characteristics of the socially-competent physician:

    ✓ Treats patients with acceptance and genuine interest

    ✓ Remains non-judgmental

- ✓ Really listens to and hears patients
- ✓ Lets anxious patients know that s/he understands their concerns
- ✓ Accepts patients as people
- ✓ Poses questions in a non-threatening way
- ✓ Looks directly at patients when talking

■ ***Step 4: Rehabilitation.*** You owe the problem partner (and, more importantly, the group itself) the opportunity for retraining and rehabilitation in behavioral factors, just as you encourage mastering a clinical weakness.

# Impose Sanctions for Continuing Problems

How to handle a partner who routinely misses deadlines for completing charts or discharge summaries? Or a member exhibiting egregious "personality" problems like constant bad temper or verbal abuse of staff and patients? Worst of all, suppose a partner's behavior borders on sexual harassment or discrimination?

Before imposing sanctions, be sure to address the problem; don't let it fester. Trouble is, no one likes to confront individual behavior issues head-on. Even when partner agreements clearly outline expectations, physicians tend to hold back from addressing violators.

### First, confront the problem

If a partner's performance jeopardizes your group's continued success, you simply can't ignore the issue. Endure the trauma of confrontation and consider these solutions, aside from the usual monetary penalties, that may work well with problem partner situations:

- *Get some help.* When you first address the problem, have one partner meet confidentially with the problem doctor. If necessary, hold a partners-only "intervention" to get across that certain behavior — like temper tantrums — affects everyone. As a last resort, require the partner to attend psychological counseling — or to take an unpaid leave of absence.

- *No work, no pay.* Hold back paychecks until the doctor has completed delinquent charts, dictation or other paperwork. Or assess a flat fine for every day late. Consider returning the fines if the offender straightens out; for example, after complying with practice guidelines for three months.

- *Work around the problem.* Reschedule a tardy physician's appointments or reassign patients to another physician for a day or two. If you compensate partners partly or wholly on production, you'll essentially cut off the offender's income in a less direct way. Plus, you'll send a strong message.

- *Plan for the worst case.* Some partner-level misdeeds like sexual, racial, religious and age-related harassment can be even worse than improper coding. Address these issues squarely in your employment and buy-sell agreements. Make it clear that the group won't tolerate such behavior and that your governing board reserves the right to terminate the doctor's employment/membership. And if the worst-case situation arises, do what the contracts say!

## How — and How Much — Can You Penalize a Non-compliant Partner?

We asked medical management consultants who work with small and mid-sized groups around the country if practices should penalize partners who present clinical or behavior problems. Their uniform answer: *Absolutely* — if you can.

If your group is typical, you've probably never even broached the idea of imposing sanctions on a partner. Even if a member truly needs the message it carries, voting to impose a monetary penalty might kick off a palace revolt that you would rather not face. Besides, perhaps your legal agreements ensure each partner his/her share of income so absolutely that you can't assess the penalty anyway.

**Serious business**

While recognizing such problems, all our experts concur: Especially with Medicare compliance rapidly becoming a major hot-button risk for physicians, even the most senior-level partner must toe the line. You simply cannot afford to let a co-owner act contrary to the group's critical interests.

Of course, don't start right out slapping penalties on a problem partner. All our experts agree that, when physicians code incorrectly, the first step is education. Be sure to specify re-training requirements in your formal compliance policy and insist on carrying it out whenever *anyone* in the office miscodes or otherwise handles duties improperly. Some physicians will consider re-training a penalty anyway, but don't back away from requiring it.

**Setting the fines**

After that, if your partner does not correct his/her ways, more drastic action becomes necessary. Don't let it slide; doing so puts you and your partners — and your practice — on the line for one who at the very least remains distracted, inattentive or just plain recalcitrant. Money penalties make sense at that point, regardless of the angst this may cause the entire group.

Don't set partner-level fines too low to have an effect. Establishing them as if they were traffic tickets won't deliver the same kick as tying compliance directly to income. A physician is too likely to shrug off small amounts like $100 or $200 without getting the message. Setting the fine too high — say, $5,000 — too often leads to a physician trying to "negotiate" the amount.

**Raise the ante**

That's why we advise establishing a *percentage fine against income* as the sole or major part of a penalty system. Consider this approach: The first offense brings a warning; the next gets a fine of 5% deducted from one's monthly income. Up the ante to 10% for each incident thereafter.

Or set a flat fine in addition to an income withhold. For example, 5% of monthly pay *plus* $100 for the first E&M violation, 5% plus $250 for the second error, and so on. Whatever figure you set, boost penalty amounts as miscoding or other adverse action continues. Don't allow any physician to just pay the "ticket" and keep on making the same mistakes.

Another approach: Establish fines as a percentage of daily base salary. Thus you might deduct one or two days' base pay for the first minor violation, then three to five days' pay for a second infraction, and so on.

These approaches emphasize a key strategy for penalizing errant members: Don't wait until the end of the year to assess fines. Unfortunately, a year-end deduction seldom improves day-to-day compliance. By reducing the non-compliant partner's pay from the very next check, you *immediately* reinforce the issue's importance.

Some offenses require an immediate *major* sanction. Sexual harassment is the classic example, as major corporations sometimes flat out and immediately respond to credible complaints against even key executives by firing or placing them on probation. The box on the next page addresses this most drastic action within a medical group.

## Be prepared!

But you cannot effectively impose penalties without paving the way. These days, effective groups' documents should specifically address performance expectations *and* permit penalizing for failure to meet them.

Most partners will back off from imposing any sort of sanctions out of the blue — even if they agree a member needs them — and the problem partner will likely fight tooth and nail if no mechanism exists for imposing them. Without clear provisions for punitive action, your chances of its having the desired remedial effect are vastly lessened. You are better served to improve your legal structure *before* a problem arises than to find yourself hamstrung when you need to act.

## Adopt a system

Unfortunately, too many practices' legal documents make it impossible to assess penalties against the co-owners. Just as bad, many practices don't address the situation at all, leaving the power totally uncertain.

> ### When All Else Fails, Vote to Expel
>
> For a partner who absolutely won't shape up, experts stress one solution: *termination*. The risk of major state or federal fines, huge uninsured court judgments (like for a sexual harassment claim) or lost managed care contracts, to name a few possible disasters, is unacceptable no matter how senior or "valuable" the partner.
>
> You may have to take a drastic measure and vote to expel the member. Is it worth the bother to go through all this? Absolutely! Having been through the issue with a number of groups in our days of consulting, we are convinced that you are far better off to endure the trauma of confrontation — and risk possible departure — than to simply tolerate a hazardous situation.
>
> When your partners almost unanimously concede in private that they would be happier without the member as a partner, that really tells you something critically important. And remember this key point: *Sometimes you grow by subtraction*.

Our experts thus urge providing for sanctions, and specifically for monetary penalties, within your group documents. Ask your attorney if your present contracts permit assessing penalties for non-compliant behavior. If they do, undertake partner-level adoption of a specific penalty system. Among other reasons, just doing so (and following it whenever necessary) helps prove the group's intent to carry out an effective Medicare compliance program — possibly mitigating any fines in case of audit.

## Assessing Medicare Fines After a Partner's Departure

It's tough enough to impose necessary sanctions on a partner who fails or refuses to follow Medicare/Medicaid coding and billing requirements. An even tougher situation occurs when a group imposes fines for penalties or miscoding — potentially huge sums — *after* the partner has retired, died or simply left the group.

Assuming the events that gave rise to the liability (i.e., the faulty coding and/or documentation occurred while the doctor was a partner), should s/he be responsible for some or all of that liability?

It depends on your inter-doctor agreements, particularly the contract that determines pay-out rights. If you can charge late-rising liabilities — which may also stem from malpractice, income tax and business dealings — against a departed partner, perhaps by reducing any payments still owed him, then you may presumably do so. If not, the partner would — barring legal action on some other basis — be secure from the problem.

## Most contracts skip the issue

Trouble is, most inter-partner contracts today are silent on the subject. Generally, such silence means that the right to payments becomes certain on the date the ex-partner retires, dies or withdraws, after which s/he owes nothing back. Events thereafter would be solely the concern of the ongoing group. Otherwise, the argument goes, a former member never knows if s/he is past that chapter of life.

Do you and your group members actually intend to immunize a departed partner from late-rising liabilities? Consider that question under two different circumstances:

(1) The partner's own improper actions gave rise to the liability.

(2) The ex-member was not directly responsible for them but, along with all the partners, s/he benefited from them.

## The departing doctor's own fault....

Suppose the now-gone member did a terrible job of documenting charts and coding procedures. In fact, perhaps s/he left the group (or was pushed out) largely because of defiance on such matters. Then a Medicare audit assesses hundreds of thousands of dollars in penalties against the practice, citing primarily (or maybe solely) claims based on the departed doctor's misdeeds.

While the auditors might proceed against that physician alone, odds are that they will assess the group as well. And it will be far easier to proceed against the practice than against the individual who may have died, retired from practice or withdrawn to live in another state or country.

That issue seems fairly clear: It calls for a contract provision that a departed partner remains responsible for claims arising specifically because of his/her own actions. If that's what your group intends, then say so right in your contracts; don't leave it open to question. You may or may not have the general right to recover or offset such liability against payments you owe, so don't leave it to chance.

### Or a group issue?

What if, instead, the fraud and abuse liability arose because of errors by the billing staff, or because your manager/administrator failed to properly train and supervise the staff, or because all or many of the doctors miscoded due to what they considered innocent misunderstanding of the E&M or surgical bundling rules? This calls for a hard policy decision among your partners.

On the one hand, when a partner leaves the group s/he becomes free of its ongoing pluses and minuses. While the practice might suffer such a later claim, it might instead receive a later bonanza: a substantial tax refund or a surprisingly large managed care bonus, for instance. Leaving the contract silent, as we said, would leave all such pluses and minuses out of the departed partner's concern. S/he could, and perhaps should, be financially removed from the ongoing group's fortunes.

On the other hand, you may feel that a partner should not profit from group activities and then escape their costs when the "piper must be paid." This view is also reasonable, especially if the piper's tune involves major matters like fraud and abuse, malpractice, large tax issues or breach of contract. If you agree this way, be sure your contracts call for charging a proportionate share of such liabilities back to the departed member.

### Reasonable approaches

Perhaps you agree with this approach but feel you should limit it to offsetting any late-rising liability against amounts you still owe the ex-partner — like stock repurchase or employee separation payments. This has the advantage of reducing and then ending the ex-partner's exposure to such claims as time passes and payments end. However, it still leaves open whether you and your partners want any exposure to survive one's retirement, death or withdrawal at all.

Both approaches are reasonable, and your group's choice should depend on how your members both work together and rely on each other. That's why we urge raising the issue for decision, even if no one ever thought about it before. Better that your arrangement be based on actual thought than on default.

# Chapter 6

*Partner Compensation*

# Adapt Your Formula to Meet Practice Goals

Not many topics can trigger strong feelings (and possibly long-lived resentment) like compensation can. Finding an objective approach to analyzing and possibly renovating your formula becomes critical.

Medical practices got off on the wrong foot many years ago by talking about income division. The term has several unfortunate connotations. For one thing, it suggests that all of a group's income will be distributed among the income-sharers. It also reinforces the presumption that whoever has produced the income gets to keep all they produced.

Further, the term calls up images of a mathematical formula that can be applied to automatically and precisely determine fair compensation for each physician's contribution. This is simplistic and often unfair. Yet once a mathematical income division formula is in place, groups will not vary from it — even to reward efforts clearly above and beyond the call of duty.

## Beware encouraging *unwanted* physician behavior

If the concept of income division itself is flawed, one aspect is most troubling: A group's formula may adversely impact physician behavior. Traditionally, groups sliced up the income pie based either upon productivity (dollars collected), equal sharing or on some combination of the two.

Disastrous behavior, from the perspective of group welfare, can result from less-than-clear-headed adoption of any such formula. Groups with 100% productivity formulas may evolve to competing more among themselves than with their real competition. But handing out equal shares of the income pie — ignoring incentive — is not necessarily any better. Rather than see the last patient, doctors may sneak off, leaving their partners to bear the burden.

## Consider key elements of group success

Despite these warts, traditional income division survives well. Many contented group practices find the right mix by blending the equal and productivity methods. Still, inequities persist; none of the methods described reward ownership and investment. Even a doctor who does not see a single patient may deserve a return on the financial investment in the practice.

Elements more essential for practice success also go overlooked. Generally, practices haven't earmarked physician leadership, executive capacity, political talents and management responsibilities for rewards. Yet these activities certainly remain critical to group success.

Undoubtedly, failure to compensate entrepreneurial effort and executive talent trace back to the days when medical practice was uncomplicated, large group practices few and lines of patients endless. Those circumstances have obviously changed. Yet physicians have been slow to adapt, and their advisors have been slow to develop new approaches.

## Different times call for different approaches

Given the upheaval engendered by managed care in its various forms, experimentation with traditional methods of compensation was clearly needed. Progressive groups refined ways to measure clinical quality, patient satisfaction, appropriate utilization and the like. Others simply continue to copy the factors that bring income to the practice.

If the HMOs pay bonuses for low emergency room utilization, few specialty referrals and lower lengths of stay, the groups incorporate those same factors into their compensation scheme. Still other groups track capitated patients to individual physicians and provide credit for episodic care on a flat dollar amount, reducing resource use and visit utilization.

We suspect, though, that no one will be able to avoid facing the enormity of the changes in the practice environment — nor the call for creativity these changes bring. Traditional income division is largely a concept of the past; compensation plans, the new order of things.

## Face it Now: One Group's Experience

Whatever formula you adopt, it's better to face the pay issue now than to wait until major payor or cost factors make their impact. "A less than perfect decision made too early is better than a perfect decision too late," says Robert A. Nelson, FACMPE, then of the Harriman Jones Medical Group in Long Beach, CA.

Harriman Jones struggled to move away from a productivity-based pay formula once it became clear its doctors' pay was no longer relating well to revenues, as the clinic was moving rapidly towards prepaid care. They switched from productivity to a flat salary arrangement. They averaged the doctors' monthly salaries over the previous 18 months and paid on that basis for the next six. The group recognized that some doctors were thus rewarded for past over-utilization, but in removing the incentive to over-utilize further, produced some cost savings.

Harriman Jones' flat salary created some negative results, too. Almost all the physicians slowed down, saw fewer patients per doctor per day, and used vacation/educational time to the fullest. Straight salaries even led the members to press for hiring more physicians, even though they weren't producing enough revenue to add doctors.

Obviously, the answer was not pure salary. Thus, the group decided to put some incentives back into its pay formula. The partners first had to figure out what they wanted to incent. The pay committee analyzed its mission statement, business plan, group culture and payor mix to identify the appropriate motivators. Ultimately, they identified seven factors:

- *Work measurement (but not just production)*
- *Quality*
- *Utilization*
- *Longevity (but do it carefully)*
- *Board certification*
- *Research and teaching activity*
- *Citizenship (positive behavior and participation)*

Ultimately, longevity, board certification and research/training fell out of the formula, though these factors may still be considered within the others. The committee added patient satisfaction, recognizing both its importance and measurability.

The remaining five factors became the basis for determining a physician-member's salary. Revenues were allocated to each specialty, and a specialty departments' salaries were set based on these criteria:
- Work completed ................ 50%  • Citizenship ......................... 10%
- Utilization .......................... 20%  • Quality ............................... 7.5%
  - Patient satisfaction ............. 12.5%

While the list is largely subjective, Harriman worked hard to quantify each factor. Even intangibles like quality and citizenship have written criteria and evaluation procedures requiring extensive calculations to set the final figure.

## Compensation Concepts

Your group's compensation formula may be its most jealously guarded sacred cow. Whether sensible or not, it continues in place as long as members don't object. And your members will likely not object as long as the pot of available income keeps growing. We expect to see still more groups struggle over partner compensation.

Despite the possible upheaval, it's time to reconsider partner pay. These five basic principles form the foundation of any income division format you design:

1. *Group members must trust the income division process and the people implementing it.*

2. *The formula must be reasonably simple and clearly understood.*

3. *The formula must provide some equity, although each member may not necessarily be treated equally.*

4. *Proper incentive to work for the growth of the group as a whole promotes practice goals.*

5. *The members must offer fair evaluations of each other and the practice's needs.*

### Four factors for revisiting your compensation plan

In light of these principles, consider the following four factors — not traditionally part of the equation — when you revisit your formula.

1. **Contribution to group success.** Producing income (productivity) remains important. But it's not the only reason why a group shows profit. Some production carries unduly high expenses; some could be due to a partner bringing in patients and referrers; and some comes from marketing efforts, physical office features, managed care contracts or hospital dominance. The key questions:

*(a)* How can your compensation plan recognize the variety of contributions partners make to *overall group success* that are not necessarily reflected in their production figures; and

   *(b)* How can your formula deal with partners who are not team players — who do their job but are otherwise a negative influence?

2. **Rewarding leadership.** As we discuss in Chapter 3, physician-level leadership is critical in determining whether a practice will succeed or fail. Typically, one person coordinates a practice's efforts. This "CEO" should give the members a sense of group purpose and ensure that everyone's marching to the same drummer. Partners may not like the idea, but they must delegate authority and accept direction from the chosen leader.

   In non-medical business settings, companies recognize the key executive's essential role in the venture's success. This normally translates to special compensation. Medical income division formulas typically fail to reward these skills and efforts, but groups cannot afford to overlook them any longer.

3. **The need for investment.** Medical groups almost universally distribute every available dollar of income to their partners; compensation formulas virtually assume and require such. New business factors contradict that old pattern. Some practices hold back substantial income to invest in state-of-the-art equipment.

   But should these deflected funds be charged against them in their old productivity formula? Should a more productive partner's income be reduced proportionately when the special expenditures will benefit all partners equally in the long run? These questions reemphasize the need for flexibility in your compensation formula.

**4. *Managed care.*** Some areas of the country remain steeped in managed care and capitation; practices *must* recognize the impact on a compensation formula. For instance, rewarding partners for the number of visits and procedures they log may be counterproductive.

Some groups split out the capitated income, less related overhead, and divide it separately from their traditional systems. With increasing data processing ability, very large groups have developed sophisticated formulas to track costs. We expect mid-sized practices to become more cost-responsive as well.

## Simplify Your Compensation Approach

No payment trend has eased the struggle to find a fair and equitable compensation method, and determining what's fair and equitable depends on who's doing the judging. For any group, the best advice is to keep it simple.

As we've said, the *differences* between practices prevent any formula from becoming the "one-size-fits-all" standard. But still, the *similarities* between most practices' revenues and expenses lead to some broad principles and model formulas adaptable almost across the board — with natural minor variations.

Atlanta health care consultant L. Michael Fleischman offers a partner compensation "template" he's found applicable in most situations. At least it serves as a good starting point for discussions on this vexing topic.

### Emphasize production

This model, diagrammed on the next page, acknowledges physician productivity's continued importance, even in these days of managed care. Professional revenue — credited to the partner that produced it — makes up the largest part of the income column. Divide all other revenue, like ancillary income and non-partner provider production (associates and non-physician providers), equally to each partner.

The basic formula then charges expenses against revenues in three ways:

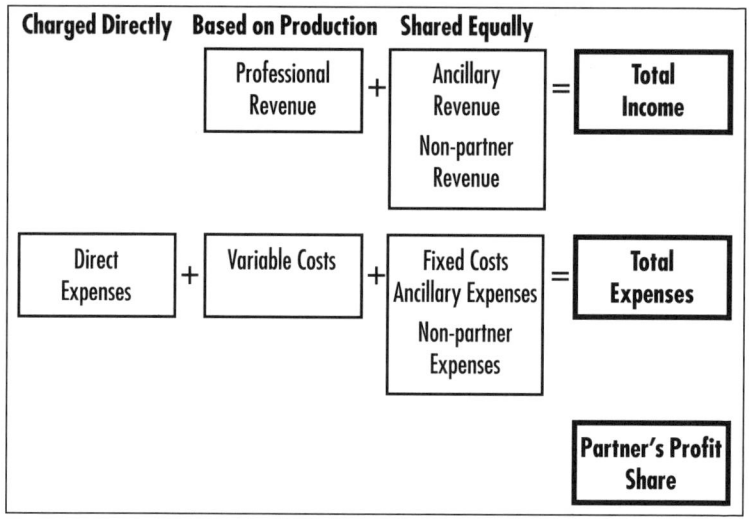

- *Direct expense.* Includes costs over which the individual partner has the most control (like personal business travel and education, books and subscriptions and even one's dedicated medical assistant's compensation). In this formula, charge such expenses to the partner dollar for dollar.

- *Variable costs.* Expenses that rise and fall with production fit into this category. Billing department salaries and benefits, for example, increase with volume since processing more charges and payments requires a larger staff. So calculate each partner's share of these expenses relative to his/her share of production. If, for instance, s/he produces one third of the revenues, then s/he bears one third of the variable expenses.

- *Equal costs.* Some business expenses, like rent and debt service, don't correspond directly to changes in patient volume. Fleischman's model formula distributes these "fixed costs" equally to all partners.

Similarly, equally allocate expenses associated with non-partners and non-physician providers — even their salaries and benefits — to reflect your equally sharing the business risks involved.

> ## Track RVU Production for Income Division
>
> Regardless of how your group measures productivity for income division, MGMA consultant Bruce A. Johnson urges keeping track of production with qualitative data. Recent surveys indicate that about 50 to 80 percent of physician groups base doctors' compensation at least partially on production.
>
> Relative value unit (RVU) data correlates sicker patient risk with higher evaluation and management codes. Payor-neutral information remains a major advantage of RVU data over other methods. If you want to measure and compare various physicians' productivity when they perform mixed services, RVUs prove a useful tool.
>
> Most practices use RVU data for billing purposes, so odds are you won't add a data collection burden. In addition to productivity, RVU data can help detect differences in practice patterns, check for coding errors, improve cost accounting and determine service efficiency. Finally, since many payors profile physicians on cost and quality of care, you'll have your own comparable data to compare against theirs.
>
> An AMA committee report cautions that using RVUs to measure physician productivity may lead to overutilization since units increase with the number of procedures and level of procedural intensity. Johnson has seen physicians gaming to rack up RVUs.
>
> Your group can get so caught up in RVU measurement that you forget to pay attention to cash, cautions Johnson. Eventually, your physicians may experience a disconnect between work and the dollars to pay the compensation.
>
> In reviewing the "better performing practices'" income division formulas, Johnson generally found "an extreme orientation to productivity." The method of measurement and specific formula you use depends on the size of your group, collection success and other factors. But look hard at using RVUs as a relatively neutral way to reflect your members' real clinical production.

## Room for discussion

The template doesn't answer all the questions. In fact, it might raise some issues you haven't thought of before. For instance, which expenses belong in each of the categories? And how do you measure productivity fairly? (Fleischman agrees that relative value units (RVUs) provide a workable standard.)

More difficult problems further complicate the picture. How, for example, can you fairly compensate a partner whose production decreases because s/he agrees to spearhead opening a new office location? Or how about a physician leader who takes time away from a busy practice to assume management/leadership work for the group?

Establishing a fair base salary for each partner may provide a partial solution. Then you would apply the profit-distribution formula only to the profit above the base. You could establish additional salary for physicians in administration or for pioneers opening new offices, too. Handling base salaries this way is more accurate and businesslike anyway, for it helps physicians recognize their basic compensation as an expense instead of a profit share.

A formula like this model may not be as useful for groups with substantial prepaid (capitated) revenue. But since most groups still collect a lion's share through (increasingly discounted) fee-for-service, you can probably adapt it to your situation.

## Managed Care Still Weighs In

Actual managed care penetration varies throughout the country, and managed care companies' specific contracts and incentives vary as well. With different practices in different stages of managed care, and the stages themselves dynamic within markets, no single compensation formula addresses all of the effects of managed care on compensation.

In fact, we, along with other health care advisors, often placed a huge emphasis on the role capitation would play in physician compensation; in some areas and practices, we were right. But the capitation stronghold in the bulk of group practices remains relatively low as a percentage of revenue, so that while it bears consideration, you might not want to base too much of your pay plan strategy on its impact.

However, under any managed care situation (which includes most practices), you should consider the impact of managed care and capitation. Medical practice recruiter and consultant Susan Cejka gives us these five helpful factors to consider:

- ■ *Production.* One way or another, a member's pay must relate to his/her contribution to profit. With fee for service, it's easy to identify: The more revenue you produce, the more you deserve to be paid.

    Under capitation, the change in what contributes to profit complicates the production component. To some extent, you'll want to encourage what Cejka calls "unproduction," yet there will be differences in doctors' levels of effort. Production of revenue — by seeing and caring for patients — is still very important, but over-treating a patient damages profits.

Consider crediting each partner with the number of patients under his/her care, multiplied by the PMPM rate. In a referral-oriented practice, it may instead be the number of patients received for new conditions, apportioned among all members' total, to determine the share of total capitated revenue. You may have to adjust for severity, requested surgical procedure or other traditional FFS factors, but limit the adjustments so there's no incentive to do more than called for.

■ *Cost Control.* Cejka favors charging costs against partners, whether the practice is capitated or not. Believing charging costs really does help control expenses, she recommends a partial cost accounting system that charges each member with the expenses s/he actually affects. They are:

*(1)* malpractice insurance premiums

*(2)* personnel directly related to the individual's practice, plus related benefits

*(3)* physician benefits

*(4)* equipment and major supplies

*(5)* office space

These five items are relatively simple to identify and allocate, and they add up to at least 70% of total overhead. Allocate the remaining indirect expenses in your previously agreed ratio, perhaps equally or in relation to total production credit.

■ *Quality.* It's questionable whether a group can pay on quality unless it can clearly measure it. Still, you can measure patient satisfaction and use available resources to produce outcomes data when possible.

Until you're comfortable with some good quality data, consider allocating perhaps 5% of group income to this factor. You may have to do it by an evaluation process, subjectively identifying each member's technical and diagnostic skills; informally observed outcome performance; and patient survey results. It may be worth including quality in your formula despite the subjectivity.

- *Citizenship.* If you want to encourage teamwork and contribution to the organization, you've got to incent it. Efforts like leadership and committee work, hospital participation and marketing really are important to the group, so don't ignore them in determining members' pay.

- *Subjective measure.* Like quality, good citizenship is subjective. Unlike quality, it always will be. The best you can do is evaluate each partner's performance and decide how much of an income pool s/he deserves under factors your members identify. Cejka suggests that no more than 5% of the group's capitated income be allocated to citizenship.

In a multi-specialty group, you must first measure between specialties. One good method pays each department an agreed PMPM amount based on the number of capitated patients in the group.

Within a single specialty group — and for a department within a multi-specialty group — you'll have to agree on a rational basis for dividing the cap rate collections. Consider exactly what incentives you want to create for this work and then apply them to your group's circumstances. Possibilities include:

- Number of capitated patients taken on by each physician (but *not* number of visits).

- Number of new patients and/or new conditions handled.

- *Limited* credit for RVUs or procedures performed, but not for tests ordered or repeat visits.

- An agreed salary or percentage, an end-of-year vote based on overall capitation effort, or a combination of agreed share plus post-agreed bonus.

## Try Three Tiers First

The consultants of one nationally active firm, The Health Care Group (HCG), tell us they often favor and end up advising a "three-tier" formula. It allows cranking in enough factors both to encourage desired behaviors and to reward members for important contributions. What should be the tiers, how to quantify them and how much relative importance to give each tier depends, of course, on the group.

Before you accuse us of telling the easy stuff and then signing off when the questions get tough, consider this breakdown:

✓ *70% for work (productivity)*

✓ *15% for executive effort (leadership)*

✓ *15% return on capital*

The work factor can be based on dollars charged or collected, hours worked or RVUs produced, but make it relatively easy to determine. The leadership factor, of course, brings into play the question of how to evaluate subjective performance, but groups must often face up to that need.

The return on capital factor typically calls for equal compensation among equal stakeholders, although young partners might phase up as a form of buy-in. Logically, though, consider making this last 15% (or whatever percentage fits your group) depend on actually having profits above some predetermined amount. Co-owners should hardly take income on a profitability factor if the enterprise didn't do well enough to justify it.

## Pick your own ratios

There is nothing magic about the 70-15-15 ratio. Your group's circumstances may properly justify 50-20-30 or 80-10-10, or whatever. Nor is there any magic in "return on capital" being a factor at all. Consider this second HCG-implemented example:

- 50% base pay (keyed largely to the prior year's production)
- 30% intangible evaluation (leadership, "citizenship," effort, patient satisfaction, etc., by an evaluation committee)
- 20% equal

And still another:

- 60% prior 12 months' relative productivity
- 30% on quality and utilization data
- 10% leadership and "citizenship" by committee evaluation process

There's nothing wrong, of course, with just two tiers in your formula. But if you're concerned about a number of priorities, avoid the temptation to weave them all into pay. Three's enough!

# Special Situations Require Special Formulas

Every practice faces special situations in compensation formulas. As we said earlier, junior and senior partners may want to approach workload differently and you'll have to adjust compensation accordingly. And when you first hire an associate, you'll structure pay differently than full partner compensation. Finally, your compensation plan should often cover pay for extra duties taken on by partners.

## Should you offer new physicians *any* incentive compensation?

Nearly two-thirds of group practices include incentive compensation in new-doctor contracts and normally base the incentive pay on physicians' (individual) productivity. The deals often define a point at which revenue from the associate's work equals the direct and indirect cost of carrying him/her. Thus, a practice with a 50% overhead ratio may give incentive pay to the extent that collections for Dr. New's services exceed twice her base salary.

A solo physician employing his first associate may then offer a bonus of half the collections for Dr. New's work exceeding twice her salary. A two-partner practice may bonus on one-third the collections over that point, and so on. The idea behind these deals is that the physicians — including the non-partner associate — will share equally in any "profits" from employing him/her. We consider an equal split of the excess too generous, but it's unfortunately fairly common.

Some practices, especially in surgical specialties, take a less generous tack. They provide an incentive only to the extent the associate's collections exceed two and a half or even three times base salary. They usually claim to have the work available for Dr. New to produce even more than that, justifying the higher productivity base on their giving away surgery that they (the present partners) would have done for their own accounts.

## Wrong incentives

We don't recommend basing the young doctor's bonus on personal productivity because it leads to group characteristics that may not serve the practice well. In fact, the very assumption that you will break even if the associate produces twice base salary is open to serious doubt.

Assume, for instance, you hire a new doctor and — as you should — seek to incorporate her into the practice by assigning many established patients and most of the new patients calling for appointments. And consider that you feed her as many of your present physician referrals as possible, promoting her to those referrers as equally capable and reliable as your seniors. In these cases, the associate's productivity may be substantial but the practice's revenue may be only somewhat greater than before she came on board.

The productivity approach starts young doctors out with more concern for their own numbers than for overall group success: it rewards building up one's own practice whether or not it builds up the group's volume.

### Better approaches

One solution to this would be to offer a bonus to the extent the *practice's* gross income increases enough to cover the new doctor's salary and costs. This rewards practice growth regardless of how much or how little you actually deflect to the associate, and it rewards the young doctor for contributing to overall growth — which should be your primary goal in adding help.

Although this solution also has drawbacks, we prefer giving the new associate an incentive to help make the overall *group* goal more profitable regardless of how his/her own scoresheet tallies up. It enables the seniors to delegate good cases as best serves the entire practice.

You can take this approach even if you and your partners divide income on relative productivity. For the first few years, it encourages your associate to contribute maximally to practice success and then join into the regular productivity format upon becoming a partner. Inserting this arrangement into the new employment contract takes some careful drafting, but it is clearly do-able.

### Salary without incentives

Our best advice: Pay a generous starting salary and provide no individual incentive compensation at all. If you recruited in order to bring on a long-term partner, don't subvert that purpose by creating a strong incentive not directly reflecting your entire goal. Producing revenue is certainly an important factor in becoming and remaining a valuable partner, but don't consider it in a vacuum.

For instance, a new doctor may be so productive simply because you gave him/her the patients and work, not necessarily "growing" the practice. A bonus merely for doing the work may detract from another important factor: creating new business. And it may depress your practice net income if the practice doesn't grow.

### Use performance evaluations to set pay

If you must offer a bonus arrangement, base it on semi-annual or annual evaluations of overall performance. Factors may include practice growth and individual effort (not just production numbers), along with a variety of criteria you ought to include in periodic evaluations anyway.

The recruit will have to trust you to be fair in such evaluations and bonus decisions, but, after all, if s/he isn't willing to trust you that far — above a generous salary — maybe you aren't such a good match anyway.

# How to Handle Compensation Questions When a Partner Wants to Cut Back

Consider these difficult group practice situations:

- A young, excellent physician you're working hard to recruit says she plans to work less than full-time.

- A non-partner associate, highly regarded as potential partner, wants to cut back her work level to have her first baby.

- A young, valued partner wants to cut back to give more time to his family, saying he will probably resume full-time practice later on.

These types of situations are common in practices nationwide. The common thread among experts we interviewed: Deal with both sexes equally when accommodating those who may become disproportionately valuable to the group.

### What's best for the *practice*

Make the accommodation because of the quality of the individuals and their value to the practice and the community, counsels Wisconsin consultant Jim Tripp. Having dealt with all three situations we pose above, he has given this advice each time, in both male and female partner requests to cut back.

If the individual is a valued practice resource, then it is in the practice's business interest to find a way to utilize that resource to its fullest, adds productivity expert Richard Haines. And more women are entering medicine, many with healthy objectives to balance a variety of interests and responsibilities, adds Michigan's Gray Tuttle. Groups who strive to accommodate these changes will prosper and stay better positioned to meet tomorrow's market demands and expectations.

### Compensation questions

While we fully agree, you still have to deal with the day-to-day reality of compensation. Atlanta's Mike Fleischman recites the story of a group in which a senior (male) partner cut back to become politically active, after which a woman came into the practice saying up front that she did not wish to work full-time. The group made similar pay arrangements for each: less than a full base salary and additional pay reflecting productivity levels.

Consultant Randy Bauman cautions that the expense factors may lead to greater adjustment since many fixed costs remain the same whether for a part- or full-timer. Malpractice insurance will not, for instance, be discounted because a physician works only 20 hours a week.

Likewise, office space, legal/accounting fees and certain staffing requirements remain the same, as well. A doctor going to 80% of full work schedule often gets less than 80% of pay, notes attorney Sandra McGraw.

From Denver, consultant Gary Thompson describes a favorite compensation based on five categories: capitation revenue, fee-for-service income, HMO/PPO fees, outside income and an allowance for covering call. Expenses are divided into fixed and variable. Then a reduced-time member can have his/her share reduced by how the factors play out in work pattern (including a fair share of expenses).

# Paying Partners for Taking on Extra Duties

Aside from your top physician leader, the increasing complexity of medical practice creates the need for physicians in all size groups to kick in with various aspects of running the practice. From sitting on an executive committee made up of less than all partners to heading an important group committee, to a major short-term job like selecting a new computer system, should one of your own receive extra pay for doing so?

Responses from trusted practice advisors around the country agree that often, for small and mid-sized groups, these extra jobs come as part of the partnership territory. But increasingly, partners begin paying for some extra duties as groups grow larger and extra duties become more critical.

## What's expected?

Naturally, serving as the group's executive or medical director normally brings some extra compensation, at least enough to make the partner whole for time away from practice. But often, physicians must serve in management roles that last a short amount of time or involve a minimal amount of their work week.

Typically partners involved in efforts to promote the practice are well reimbursed for their expenses but not compensated for their time. When every partner absorbs an equal burden, no additional compensation is necessary.

Everybody in a practice might spend about 20 to 30 hours a year on administrative meetings or community work, but when a partner goes above and beyond the equal burden, the formula gets trickier. Practice management advisor Jack Valancy offers the example of a computer system purchase: When a doctor heads the effort, leads vendor selection and communication, works with staff and consultants, and oversees installation, you're looking at a lot of time away from the practice over a short term.

## Fair market value?

Many groups distribute at least some income to recognize "partner" status, essentially like a share of profits. Partner status calls for assuming group duties. But groups evolve and duties often become less-equally distributed over time. Those changed circumstances may call for compensating members who take on burdens that others either avoid or handle less well.

When that happens, most groups base administrative time on an equivalent scale to actual production time. Advisor Gray Tuttle works with a group that uses RVUs to measure productivity. With the exception of some intensity factors, it's a time-oriented approach; all partners offset RVU production lost to administrative duties with equivalent pay.

Other groups might pay for extra administrative duties, but not necessarily at "fair market value." Valancy suggests paying up to 80% of regular earnings for extra administrative work. Paying moderately to "legitimize" a partner's undertaking might come in the form of a stipend, provided s/he attends required meetings and fulfills the duties.

No matter the formula, treat this extra pay as a practice expense *before* determining income shares. This way, the work becomes recognized for what it is — something outside a regular partner's divisible income — and the group can evaluate whether the pay is fair for the work performed.

**Valuing extra duties**

Keep in mind, administration outcomes don't measure like clinical outcomes and it's difficult to convert administrative worth to dollars. Most experts agree that medical groups must pay attention to the business side of practice and physicians must be involved. That's why many experts stress that "group mentality" emphasizes doing your share of extra duties for the common good.

However, when your needs require more than the normal turn, remember that all members benefit from the efforts of those who spend extra time and expertise on important business-related matters. Think of paying for that effort much as if you hired and paid an outsider.

Successful physicians learn to strike a good balance between clinical and administrative efforts. Still, most physicians prefer to spend their time on clinical practice and typically the ones with the skills and interest end up doing the extra administrative work. So when you think that work goes above and beyond typical partner expectations, be open to paying fairly for it.

# An Online Tool to Help Evaluate Your Physician Pay Plan

MGMA consultants Robert C. Bohlmann, FACMPE and Bruce A. Johnson, JD, MPA have created an interactive questionnaire for group practices based on generally-effective principles of successful plans. While their online assessment tool won't tell you what's right or wrong with your compensation plan or invent the "right" plan for your group, it will help you conduct a fairly thorough discussion among your partners. And if you're considering hired help, you can use this tool before your outside expert arrives; it may save billable hours and make his/her efforts more productive, too.

The consultants' self-assessment tool presents a battery of questions in 12 sections dealing with nearly every aspect of a physician compensation system. Here are the key topics:

***1.*** *Current system strengths, weaknesses and features.* Besides giving you a chance to reflect on what's good and bad about your system, this section asks about such features as measuring physician productivity and whether you use data benchmarks to compare with other practices.

***2.*** *Compensation system goals.* First, it asks you to state your pay plan's goals — in other words, what should your formula encourage and reward? Then it asks whether or not the system really accomplishes the stated goals.

***3.*** *Historical change.* Often a practice carves its pay plan in stone and never updates plan guidelines to reflect changes in its situation. This section challenges you to consider how your practice environment has changed over the past three years.

***4.*** *Physician demographics.* This part calls on you to list your physicians by age grouping. Physicians' ages generally influence their income expectations and consequently, their (dis-) satisfaction with the pay system.

***5.*** *Call coverage.* The questionnaire asks whether your system allows for a physician to modify his/her call participation under certain circumstances, like approaching retirement.

***6.*** *Outside income and activities.* Here it explores your group's policies and attitudes about non-medical revenue generated by the physicians (like honorariums or expert testimony fees).

***7.*** *Time off.* Questions about time-off policies and practices.

***8.*** *Part-time and partial retirement physicians.* Does your plan accommodate anything less than "full-time"?

***9.*** *Authority over practice resources and expenses.* These questions explore your group's policies regarding the extent of individual physicians' authority to spend practice money, hire personnel or purchase equipment. If they have such personal control, how are those expenses shared?

***10.*** *Performance feedback mechanisms.* This part asks primarily about production measures and reports to physicians. But it also asks whether you have stated performance expectations for the doctors, too.

***11.** Practice culture.* This section approaches how your physicians define what they consider to be "fair." What does it mean to be part of a *group*?

***12.** Compliance.* It simply asks whether your pay plan complies with anti-self-referral (Stark) regulations.

To assess your group's plan, go to *www.mgma.com/pract_solutions/* and scroll down the screen to "A compensation system self-assessment tool."

# Chapter 7

*Legal Issues*

# New Stark II Revision
# Finally Clears Up Major Questions

Even if productivity remains sensible for your group, you risk violating federal self-referral laws if your formula includes credit for ordering certain ancillary services. Fortunately, the final Stark II rule issued January 2001 helps clarify many previously cloudy interpretations of federal law.

The first self-referral law arose in the 1980s, when a government study alarmed Congress with reports that physicians holding financial interests in clinical labs ordered far more lab work than those with no stake in the labs. By 1989, Congress reacted by passing the so-called "Stark" law (after its sponsor Rep. Fortney "Pete" Stark, D-CA) prohibiting physicians from referring Medicare or Medicaid patients to labs in which they or family members held a financial stake. In 1993, Congress amended and expanded the law (Stark II) to include 10 other designated health services (DHSs).

## Defining Designated Health Services

At more than 600 pages, the 2001 final rule goes to great lengths to clarify DHS definitions, as listed in the box on the next page. These clarifications form the core of the latest ruling and are important enough that we present them separately in a special section at the end of this chapter (**see page 101**). But while the DHS definitions have garnered the greatest attention, they're not the only Stark II elements affecting profitable (and fully legal) group practice. The amended rule also details how your group must operate, who else it may affiliate with, how it designates partners and how it shares revenues.

## Designated health services (DHSs)

- Clinical laboratory services
- Physical therapy services
- Occupational therapy services
- Radiology services (including MRI, CT scans and ultrasound)
- Radiation therapy services (and supplies)
- Durable medical equipment (DME) and supplies
- Parenteral/enteral nutrients, equipment and supplies
- Prosthetics, orthotics and prosthetic devices and supplies
- Home health services
- Outpatient prescription drugs
- Inpatient/outpatient hospital services

## Defining a 'Group'

Under the Stark II general exemption for "physician services" you can refer an otherwise-prohibited service (a DHS) within your group. Since HCFA made this group-practice exemption, it had to clearly define what it considers a bona fide "group," too.

Thankfully, the new final rule uses fairly realistic criteria and provides an understandable definition. According to HCFA, a medical group can practice in more than one building, but in that case the group must show the following attributes:

✓ "Centralized decision-making" by a representative body having control over assets and liabilities (including budgets, compensation and salaries)

✓ Consolidated billing, accounting and financial reporting and centralized utilization review

✓ "Substantially all" (at least 75%) of the group's patient care rendered by "members" (i.e., group employees/owners as opposed to independently contracted physicians)

The originally-proposed rule had made it nearly impossible for "group practices without walls" to qualify for the in-office ancillary exception. But happily, the final rule's guidelines clearly allow for such arrangements (if they also meet the other criteria).

**Independent contractors**

Not only must group members provide 75% of patient care services, but 75% of their practice must take place within the group. So if members provide patient care (and submit bills) through another entity, their "moonlighting" must not exceed 25% of their professional activity.

These rules allow for independent contractor arrangements without jeopardizing group status. They permit, for example, a group with mammography equipment to contract with a radiologist for interpreting the films. The group could pay the radiologist a flat stipend for reading films, then submit claims for both technical and professional components. (Of course, have qualified legal counsel review *any* independent contractor deals before you sign an agreement. Some of the details can get tricky.)

## Sharing the Profits

But how can a group legally distribute profit generated by its DHS technical components? Hoping to eliminate any financial incentives for physicians to order more (or more expensive) designated health services, HCFA produced fairly complicated rules covering how medical groups may distribute DHS profits. The allowable profit-sharing formulas center around a single theme: No physician may receive compensation directly or indirectly related to the volume or value of his/her Medicare DHS referrals.

HCFA defines "referral" as any service *not* performed personally by the ordering physician. So, for example, when a physician reads an x-ray s/he ordered for a patient, that "professional component" falls outside the definition. But you must consider the "technical component" (TC), even when performed by a supervised employee, a referral. HCFA sees it as a service you ordered, to be provided by someone else.

So unless physicians *personally* perform x-ray procedures themselves, your group cannot distribute revenues or profits from TCs based on who ordered the film. Even so, the final rule does allow distributing the overall profits from Medicare DHSs on any "reasonable and verifiable" basis not directly related to each physician's referrals.

## 'Safe' approaches

The simplest way to comply with Stark on this issue is to divide profits from the technical components equally among group members. If your group uses a productivity-based compensation formula, you can just add an equal share of the DHS TC revenue to each physician's production before completing the calculation.

The final rule allows for unequal profit distribution, too. You may distribute DHS profits based on *other* productivity like office visits or surgery and procedure revenues, but you may not include *any* DHS revenue — even non-Medicare DHS revenue — when calculating share proportions.

Our table on below shows how this kind of formula would work. Each physician's professional revenue (say, collections) appears in column B. Column C shows each one's share (as a percentage) of the overall physician services revenue. Columns D and E show the revenue produced by each physician's actual lab orders.

### Tracking the technical component

Column F of the table displays the Medicare/Medicaid lab revenue — redistributed by each physician's share of non-lab revenue (column C). The last column (G) shows the adjusted revenue for calculating each physician's compensation (the sum of columns B, E and F).

### Sample Stark-compliant formula calculation

| Physician | Professional Revenue | | Actual In-Office Lab Revenue | | Medicare DHS Revenue Redistributed (C x Sum of D) | Total Revenue Credited for Formula Calculation |
| | | | Medicare/ Medicaid | All Other Payors | | |
| | Dollars | % | Dollars | Dollars | | |
| [A] | [B] | [C] | [D] | [E] | [F] | [G] |
| Dr. Green | $27,000 | 36.5% | $480 | $1,300 | $608 | $28,908 |
| Dr. Brown | $21,000 | 28.4% | $537 | $1,547 | $473 | $23,020 |
| Dr. Black | $26,000 | 35.1% | $650 | $1,821 | $586 | $28,407 |
| TOTAL: | $74,000 | | $1,667 | $4,668 | $1,667 | $80,335 |

Tracking the technical component dollars in your information system may require making changes in the way your billing staff enters charges, payments and adjustments. Check with your computer vendor to find out its recommended way to handle the data.

Finally, HCFA wisely made an allowance for practices with negligible Medicare/Medicaid DHS revenue. The final rule states that if the practice's total DHS revenue doesn't exceed 5% of its total revenue (*and* each physician's share of the DHS revenue doesn't exceed 5% of his/her total revenue), then you can include the DHS revenue in your regular profit distribution formula without jeopardizing your group status.

## Address Partners' Conflicts of Interest

"Conflict of interest" is a business term; like "insider trading," we typically associate it with big corporations. But conflicts can also occur in medical practices when a partner puts — or could put — a non-group interest before the good of the group.

Physicians these days assume a variety of roles within and outside medicine. Healthcare consultant and attorney Janice Cunningham finds doctors confronted with conflicts they never expected. For instance, whether willingly or reluctantly, they assume managerial positions within integrated delivery systems, PHOs and HMOs that sometimes negotiate deals contrary to their own group's best interests. And any arrangement involving a hospital signals a potential conflict.

### Multiple roles

Physicians may not recognize their legal responsibilities when they assume roles in multiple organizations. As an officer/director of any corporation, and as a partner within any partnership, you carry a fiduciary responsibility to that entity to act for it as a reasonable businessperson. Remember, physicians owe this fiduciary duty not only to their group but to other entities they serve.

Consider the experience of a large multi-specialty group with physicians practicing at three hospitals. Serving on the Board of one hospital's PHO, a physician-partner approved an exclusive contract with a dominant payor. Though a great coup for the PHO, the contract cut off some of his partners from a critical patient population. That physician had a serious conflict.

To clarify physician obligations and forestall various potential problems, Cunningham counsels adopting a *written* policy on conflicts of interest. Make sure it requires your members at least to:

- ✓ Disclose any potential conflict of interest
- ✓ Divulge any material facts concerning business decisions
- ✓ Request approval for all outside business activities

### Discuss it — and maybe decline to serve

Should the partner serving on the PHO board abstain from voting on any PHO decision that might affect his/her group? Perhaps, but s/he then functions as a less-effective PHO board member. At the very least, partners ought to discuss all outside commitments that involve serving "another master" or "wearing another hat."

If your group requires an exclusive commitment, it may limit your participation in outside organizations, thus reducing your group's influence on these entities and diminishing your access to information. But that may be the price of avoiding potentially messy conflicts of interest.

### Personal conflicts

Conflicts can also occur on a more personal level when partners can or do put self-interest before the group's well-being. Say your practice needs computer software. One partner pushes a product offered by a company in which he has invested. As a corporate officer he has a duty to disclose his outside interest and potential conflict.

You can certainly consider the interested partner's input. But prohibit him/her from participating in the decision. The best decision comes from independent evaluation by impartial partners.

## Up Front, Not Under the Table

Partners must also disclose all material facts they know that may affect any business issue. Cunningham recalls how one physician, sole owner of the space leased to his group, knew that property values and rental rates in the area had dropped during the group's five-year lease. He proposed renewing at the same rate, and his unsuspecting partners signed the lease.

As a matter of law, partners may not withhold information affecting group business, especially for their own self-interest. Taking advantage of colleagues by not telling them all the facts destroys the basic trust needed for partners to function as a group.

There's no "magic bullet" solution for conflict issues like these; every situation is unique. But heed this one clear lesson:

> Discuss all potential conflict of interest matters as soon as they even suggest themselves. Conflicts coming to light later can too easily result in group disintegration or inter-partner legal action.

*Chapter 7: Legal Issues*

# Final Stark II Designated Health Services Definitions and Exemptions

The January 2001 revision of the final Stark II guidelines should prove significantly more definite than past releases in helping group practices steer clear of self-referral infractions and penalties. In a nutshell, the newest rulings clarify these important federal definitions:

- **Physician services.** Referring to another physician in the same group for personally-performed medical care does not come under Stark's self-referral prohibition. But make sure the practice qualifies as a medical "group" under Stark guidelines.

- **In-office ancillary services.** Such services furnished by the physician, a fellow group member or a physician-supervised employee in the office are not considered DHSs. Our chart on the next page breaks out the basic criteria for determining if ancillary services qualify as "in-office."

For five DHS categories, HCFA lists specific procedures by CPT code. Those listed in the box **on page 101** are subject to Stark II. Thus CPT codes *not* specifically listed are not considered DHSs under Stark.

## Specific exemptions

The procedure lists marked "excluded" are services that HCFA will *not* consider DHSs for Stark purposes. You may order and perform those procedures (and be reimbursed) free of Stark restrictions. The regulations provide for other exemptions, too, including these significant ones:

- ■ *Specialty-specific services.* For many specialties, HCFA declared a number of common procedures exempt. For example, oncologists can provide external ambulatory infusion pumps for chemotherapy and pain medication under the "in-office ancillary" exception. Urologists can administer Medicare-paid PSA tests as an exempted "preventive screening" test. But make sure your diagnosis coding reflects symptoms or history, cautions Jeri Harris, CPC-H. Medicare won't usually pay for routine screenings.

- ■ *Tests, immunizations/vaccines.* Medicare-paid flu, Hepatitis B and pneumococcal vaccines have a special exemption. Further, HCFA specified the following as exempt, too:

- ✓ EKG
- ✓ PFT
- ✓ EEG
- ✓ Stress tests
- ✓ Holter monitor
- ✓ Nuclear medicine studies
- ✓ Post-cataract glasses or contact lenses
- ✓ Ancillary services administered at ambulatory centers. If the physician supplies an implant — like intraocular lenses or a cochlear implant — at an ambulatory center, HCFA considers them exempt. The same applies to dialysis-related drugs administered at an end-stage renal disease facility.
- ✓ Durable medical equipment (DME). Physicians can provide blood glucose monitors for home use under the "in-office" exception. And HCFA has provided exemption for canes, crutches, walkers and folding wheelchairs dispensed in the office — as long as the physician is a certified DME provider.

Remember, you can order and perform exempted procedures *as described above* without concern for Stark prohibitions.

### Criteria for determining if a service qualifies under the in-office ancillary services exemption

| WHO | WHERE | IF |
|---|---|---|
| Personally by referring physician | In the same building[1] where the referring physician usually practices | The patient did not contact the referring physician *primarily* to receive designated health services |
| OR<br>Personally by another physician in the same group | OR<br>In a centralized building[2] used exclusively by the referring physician's group practice | AND<br>The referring physician or the medical group bills for the services using their individual/group provider numbers |
| OR<br>By an individual supervised by the referring physician or another physician in the same group | [1] "Same building" means structure or group of structures sharing the same address.<br>[2] "Centralized building" means all or part of a building owned or leased full-time and used exclusively by the group practice (for at least 6 months). | |

# Chapter 8

*Arrangements for Departing Members*

# Include Provisions for the Good of the Departing Member and the Group

When a physician leaves the group, the paramount concern is the practice's ability to continue as a successful business caring for the same patients, both before and after the departure. Protecting ongoing earning capacity typically involves a *restrictive covenant*, a *non-solicitation agreement* and a *non-disclosure agreement*.

Physicians have long loathed restrictive covenants, but these arrangements prove critical to maintaining a practice's business against a physician-member leaving to compete. While prohibited in some states, a reasonably-crafted restrictive covenant is in most cases the only sure way to protect the practice's patient base.

## Preventing *patient* departures

The second item of protection, a non-solicitation agreement, prohibits a departing physician from asking the practice's patients to follow to a new practice. The agreement should also require the leaving doctor not to steal the practice's employees or managed care or other service agreements, and not solicit to the practice's referral base.

Finally, more agreements these days have clauses prohibiting the disclosure of confidential information. If the practice develops a favorable contract with a managed care organization, make sure a departing doctor cannot convert that information to his/her new practice's advantage.

Another issue in connection with physician departures: the path to full retirement. Many groups require each member, regardless of age or years of service, to bear all of a full partner's burdens. Allowing members to phase into retirement helps ensure moving senior members' relationships in an orderly fashion to the continuing members. Those relationships certainly include patients, but may just as importantly include business contacts, referral relations and hospital political connections.

### Design a reasonable pay-out provision

Generally, little can be done to prepare for death or disability. Perhaps the best insurance is a well-devised pay-out program, coupled with a sound business plan. The pay-out must be designed to avoid strapping the ongoing practice for cash. The business plan plots how the practice will run even if a tragedy should strike.

Regardless of the reason for departure, pay-outs require careful consideration. An appropriate pay-out ensures that the former colleague is reasonably compensated for the practice left behind, while at the same time the ongoing group is neither strapped financially nor the beneficiary of a windfall.

Treading between those two positions can be difficult. Though heavily debated, medical practice goodwill values clearly exist. But how much in any particular case? Should the leaving doctor be entitled to a fixed sum? Or should that sum be subject to variation if the practice's future economics head south? Should there be any recalculation of a leaving doctor's payment if shortly after departure the practice is sold for much more than expected?

### Selling 'outside' the practice

This last question became vexing in the late 1990s, as more groups sold their practices to hospitals, insurance companies and management firms. Few arrangements adequately dealt with distribution of sale proceeds, leading to a new partner's possibly receiving the same portion of the sales price as a founding member. Though such high-price sale scenarios have mostly abated, they show the need for care in drafting pay-out agreements.

In sum, the answers to all the questions posed above — and to the other issues swirling around physician departures — are never altogether clear. Nonetheless, with good forethought, inevitable changes in a group's physician complement can be handled with grace and fairness.

# Restrictive Covenants

We strongly support including protection against competitive practice in all partners' arrangements. A restrictive covenant on your existing partners is important to governing the practice for its own success.

For starters, if you don't impose such restrictions on yourselves, you will find it difficult to justify them to young doctors you bring into membership. You may have the negotiating clout to insist on them anyway, but it's only good practice to have the same clause for yourselves, whether you like it or not.

In addition, having the restriction apply to all says that the group is more important than any partner. As we discussed in Chapter 4, many groups flounder because they accommodate their partners' varied priorities rather than their best organizational goals.

The solution: Make all partners subject to restrictive covenants. Yet even if logical and correct, this advice may not convince a partner to surrender present freedom to stay or leave at will. After all, who wants to give up that security and become subject to the decisions of others? But if you recognize that your long-term security depends on group success, you may have to accept restrictions.

A non-compete agreement can serve as a sort of litmus test for a group's resolve — and taking the agreement seriously can help you endure non-unanimous votes and non-compliant physicians. Remember, if anyone can leave at any time for any reason, you're really not a group, advises practice consultant Randy Bauman. Consider his illustrative parable in the box **on page 109.**

## New associates and existing partners

Imposing non-compete covenants on newly recruited physicians is nowadays standard procedure. Partners in established groups recognize the folly of paying a salary and expenses while the new doctor builds a reputation and referral base that s/he can take down the road. Unless your state laws won't enforce it, don't let even the most impressive candidate negotiate out of a non-compete restriction.

We also encourage groups to revisit non-compete provisions whenever they make significant investments, such as building a new office or adding expensive ancillary services (like CT or MRI).

Getting existing partners to sign such an agreement, or to ac-

> ## Contribution Vs. Commitment
>
> The collapse of hospital employment and physician practice management corporation models has increased resistance to strict non-competes. Many physicians and their practices must make significant investments to reacquire assets and re-establish their practices, leaving them to resist tying themselves up legally all over again.
>
> For those facing a restructure, or groups just revisiting their non-compete arrangements, Bauman emphasizes the difference between contribution and commitment with the example of the ham and eggs breakfast: "The chicken made a contribution and the pig made a commitment."

cept a more restrictive version, may prove even more difficult. But in order for such covenants to hold up in court, they really must be consistent among all group members.

Small practices merging into larger groups especially find the non-compete agreements a bitter pill to swallow. Small groups rarely have their own restrictions, and members sometimes obstruct deal closure by refusing to sign off their freedom.

### Emphasize commitment

You need some sort of "glue" mechanism, but if the covenant poses overly strict rules, it won't fly for all members. For instance, one group decided on a very narrow restriction from competing for one year after withdrawal and within five miles of the practice. It didn't really do much more than stop a departing physician from practicing across the street, as Bauman points out.

Another group included a provision to require departing members to pay their share of central office overhead for a period of two years. This seems a variant of a buy-out penalty when a partner leaves the group to compete, but paying a share of overhead follows the logic above — that the group is making financial decisions based on the assumption that everyone is committed to the practice together.

An agreement that makes a departing physician pay the prorate share of debt through reduction in their pay-out is, by itself, often insufficient because the overhead and other practice commitments still remain. Buy-out penalties are still used and often groups extend the pay-out term to five years or longer; at least that way, the group doesn't finance a future competitor's start-up.

### Insist on it

How to handle any partner's refusal to sign depends on your circumstances. In almost every case, however, physicians tend to think of non-compete provisions from a personal standpoint — their own departure.

Remind these doctors to put themselves in the remaining members' position. Once their frame of reference changes to being left with investment in infrastructure, overhead and the debt without the partner to carry it, their positions tend to change. Many say, "I came in here dead-set against a non-compete, but now I think it's important that we have one."

Finally, the best deterrent to physician departure remains financial success. Bauman cites a group with significant ancillary services and physician income approaching 200% of national averages. The group operates well without a non-compete — because, as Bauman notes, why would anyone *want* to leave?

## Are Restrictive Covenants Enforceable?

As a matter of general law, restrictive covenants are legally enforceable if they are "reasonable." For the most part, this includes reasonableness to the public (no shortage of physicians in the specialty, for example), to the continuing practice, and to the departing doctor. Essentially, they exist to protect the ongoing practice's legitimate business concern while not becoming unfair to the departing doctor or the general public.

A number of states have laws on the books protecting against restrictive covenants of physician-employee situations. In these states, you would be wise to seek legal advice on how to satisfy state law provisions, but still include restrictions.

### General enforceability

In most states no special laws govern restrictive covenants. So can you guarantee that the restrictive covenant in your partner's or associate's contract will be enforced if brought to court?

Unfortunately, no. A judge still has wide latitude in deciding how to handle a case involving a physician's departure and competition, even in the face of a clearly stated and signed prohibition.

To enforce a restriction against a departing partner, your lawyer will first seek a "preliminary injunction" requiring that s/he stop the competitive activity until your case can actually be heard under the court's calendar. It's impossible to predict how a judge will decide the preliminary request, for the law gives broad judiciary discretion at this stage. If the court does not grant immediate relief, your former partner may continue to compete at least until the case is heard and decided — perhaps for years after leaving you.

## Use them anyway

Does all this uncertainty mean you need not bother to insert strong restrictive covenants in your new doctor and interpartner agreements? Absolutely not! Unless clearly unenforceable in your state, we strongly recommend including — and if need be, acting upon — well drafted contract prohibitions.

Even with the legal uncertainty, your practice is better protected with such restrictions than without them. Court decisions still leave the basic law on your side — permitting proper restrictions unless some facts convince a judge to decide differently. At the very least, this gives you real flexibility in deciding how to react to the new competition.

The vast majority of restrictive covenant cases are settled or decided at the lower court (usually unpublished) level, often in favor of the ongoing practice, points out health care attorney and consultant Sandra McGraw. Remember, too, that your new competitor will be subject to the same legal uncertainties that puzzle you. Leaving your practice and opening a competing office in the face of a restrictive covenant entails great risk. And that risk comes at a time when s/he may be least able to afford it. Thus, at least partly due to the contract restrictions, most situations result in the departing doctors choosing new careers that are *not* competitive.

Besides, the times virtually demand protecting your practice against a former partner's inroads. Patient and referring doctor relationships are hard enough to maintain, and volume is critical as payors reimburse less than in the past. And what if your new competitor takes over important contract relationships — a managed care contract or a hospital arrangement, for instance — which supply you with significant *blocks* of patients? You need the protection regardless of how you ultimately use it.

Consult your attorney about your state's law for guidance in structuring restrictive covenants. If your regular lawyer isn't enthusiastic about restrictions or is not experienced in dealing with and enforcing them, seek a second opinion. There's too much at stake to do less.

## Partial Retirement

Many years ago, we urged groups to make advance plans for a senior member's phase-down. Since then, many doctors have decided to pull back without entirely leaving practice. A cutback in the seniors' work and pay may suit the younger members, as well. So our advice holds up: Plan now for semi-retirement or regret it later.

In some groups, younger partners increasingly favor their senior partners' flat out retiring. Declining patient flow and revenues, especially in some specialties, make the younger members less tolerant of their seniors' discomfort. But most of these single-specialty groups remain busy enough that a senior's continued practice serves them well. If still fee-for-service-dominated, they may value his/her referral ties and reputation. And the senior often provides needed leadership and political strength.

Discussing how a partner can slow down in preparation for full retirement requires the same kind of cool thinking and advanced planning. So provide for a "phase-down" policy for group members long before you need it.

### Ask these questions

At issue are two questions: How do you accommodate a senior's desire to continue practicing good medicine at a lesser pace? And how do you avoid compromising younger members' profitability while undergoing such a drastic change? As with most group matters, there's no simple partial retirement formula that works for everyone.

Considering your group's unique circumstances, allow members at a specified age and/or years of service to propose a phase-down plan. Require the applicant to present it at least six months before the proposed effective date, after which the partners must vote on the plan within two months. Approval is for only a year at a time; the senior must reapply the same way — including six months early — each year to repeat (or modify) the arrangement.

### The big issues

The proposal for partial retirement must include several big issues for the group to approve, reject or make a counter offer. The applicant must propose a specific work schedule as well as a salary or income share for the changed workload. When it's your turn to apply, don't set your expectations too high in these days of reduced reimbursements and high overhead.

Fit the plan to your own compensation formula. If the group pays heavily on productivity, the cutback in activity can provide a "natural" pay reduction. But build in safeguards against gaming the system. Don't allow a partially-retired doctor to simply become more selective in taking better-paying patients. Be sure, too, that fixed practice expenses remain charged to the semi-retiree. Reduced production doesn't decrease these costs.

### Call duty

Almost as difficult as the compensation question, be careful in outlining the details of the reduced physician activity. Is s/he going to limit office hours? Does it make sense to narrow the senior's case mix to a few favorite procedures? And, of course, what about night and weekend call?

The larger your group, the better it can handle a member's reduction in call participation. A smaller group may simply have to require call duty as the price of being a member — even part-time. And remember the bottom line: *The needs of the group must take priority over any member's personal goals.*

If you determine that your group can allow a member to reduce or eliminate call, come up with a sensible plan for reducing compensation accordingly. How to be fair in doing that varies greatly between specialties and groups. It helps to find out what similar group practices have done, but don't take others' plans as gospel; we've seen too many half-baked methods.

### Part-time partners?

A senior member in phase-down should probably give up legal co-owner status. Today's pressures on medical practices call for tough decisions about the future. "Business as usual" usually won't cut it. That's why many top advisors recommend requiring less-than-full-time partners to sell out. Hard decisions demand strong commitment and a vested interest in the future.

Often, however, a group's documents calculate a departing physician's pay-out amount based on his/her last year of production. If s/he enters a phase-down period, consider "freezing" the last full-production year as the calculation base. Then defer paying the frozen amount until full retirement.

Finally, when you amend your organizational documents to include a phase-down plan, set an absolute time limit — perhaps five years — for continuing the part-time status. At the end of that period, make full retirement mandatory. Otherwise the "end-stage" plan could drag on indefinitely and hamper the group's ability to move forward with future plans.

The population "bubble" made up of baby boomers has already reached age 50. And if your group is typical, you don't have much time to prepare for the coming wave of retirements. Don't keep putting off sensibly planning for what you'll inevitably have to face.

## Put it in writing

Once you decide on a format, officially adopt it in writing. Include the rules in your formal legal documents, either partnership agreement or corporate employment contracts. Or else, at an official members' meeting, adopt a written resolution to be incorporated into an informal Summary of Members' Benefits. Give the summary to each member and redistribute it each year as a reminder.

An important item to consider as you decide on a format: How will you handle the senior's pay-out upon full retirement?

This deserves special consideration, both out of fairness and to encourage an orderly transition from phase down to over-and-out. The fact that one stops practicing in stages — over several years rather than all at once — shouldn't logically change the entitlement.

## Phase down and freeze pay-out

Consider, for example, a senior doctor reducing his/her activity by 20% per year for five straight years. If your regular pay-out formula, likely premised on immediate and total cessation of practice, is based on the last year's pay, s/he would receive only 20% of the expected pay-out when actually retiring at the end of the fifth year. Yet over the five years of semi-retirement, the senior would cumulatively leave behind the same value as another partner receives by retiring all at once.

The solution: Freeze the retirement pay-out on the date the member starts phasing down activity, subject to all the customary protective limitations you place on future pay-outs. This partially retiring physician will thus receive a full distribution as if retiring, deferred until the final departure from the group. It's easy to provide for such a frozen distribution by amending the group's documents when you make the partial-retirement decision.

## Full Retirement or Other Departure

Of course, the reasonableness and affordability of pay-outs for departing partners, be they phasing down or fully retiring, causes great concern. Do long-standing partner payout formulas still make sense? Should we downsize our partners' pay-outs? Younger group members worry that a senior partner's departure will trigger payments too generous for the times. They point to managed care, falling reimbursements and other troubling trends as proof that the formula agreed to years ago must now be scaled down.

We wish there was one right answer for all, but, alas, there isn't. Instead, each group must review arrangements thoroughly, starting with goodwill value. To get you started, health care consultant and attorney Daniel Bernick suggests a simple reality check.

### Goodwill value

The first step is to determine the practice's intangible goodwill value, a tricky and sensitive issue. Some young doctors argue that goodwill value no longer exists as a financial factor at all. However, it is still an accepted asset that must not be ignored.

A typical pay-out arrangement comprises two parts. First is a repurchase of the departing member's corporate stock keyed to the value of the practice's hard assets (such as furniture, equipment and office build-outs). For most practices these values are relatively modest and not in dispute.

Most of a pay-out lies in the second part of the deal, usually called separation pay or deferred compensation. Typically paid over three to five years to recognize the departing member's interest in the group's accounts receivable and goodwill value, it essentially rewards the doctor for past contribution to practice success.

## Estimating goodwill value

Though calculation methods differ, it's fairly straightforward to place a value on tangible assets like real estate, equipment, furniture and accounts receivable. Once you agree to a reasonable formula, arriving at the value is just a math problem.

But what about the intangibles — what the business world calls "goodwill?" Shouldn't a buyer recognize real value in your years of sacrifice and hard work? Don't the things that make your practice a "going concern" count for something? Certainly there must be value in your good name!

The best starting point in determining goodwill: a good database. Since 1985, The Health Care Group (HCG), a consulting firm in Plymouth Meeting, PA, has collected statistics from actual medical practice transactions across the country and published them in its annual *Goodwill Registry*.

The *Registry* expresses each reported practice's goodwill value as a percentage of gross collected revenue (before expenses) and breaks out the data by medical specialty. In 15 years it has become the standard source where you can find the *range* of goodwill values reported for practices similar to your own. The most current HCG *Goodwill Registry,* shown on page 115, reports goodwill values of buy-ins, pay-outs, practice sales and appraisal reports across the country. Use it as a benchmark.

# Defining Goodwill

Even though we've heard credible advisors say, "No one really pays for goodwill anymore," practices indeed fetch a price exceeding the value of their hard assets. Ohio health care attorney Peter Pavarini casually defines goodwill as the amount the purchase price exceeds the identifiable assets, net of assumed liabilities.

Goodwill is the likelihood that patients will continue to return to a medical practice because it has all the right business and operational systems in place. Attorney Sandra McGraw and consultant Michael Parshall offer examples such as:

## General Benchmarks for Goodwill Values*

| Specialty | Goodwill | No Goodwill | Mean | Median | Low | High |
|---|---|---|---|---|---|---|
| Primary Care | 1222 | 129 | 35.24% | 30.77% | 0.03% | 405.69% |
| OB/Gyn | 231 | 31 | 32.80% | 28.89% | 0.40% | 117.19% |
| Ophthalmology | 195 | 20 | 36.70% | 34.39% | 0.03% | 140.08% |
| Otolaryngological surgery | 48 | 14 | 36.00% | 25.00% | 0.11% | 318.45% |
| Internal medicine subspecialties | 162 | 51 | 33.81% | 29.89% | 0.67% | 220.98% |
| Surgical practices | 270 | 80 | 30.60% | 25.78% | 0.11% | 318.45% |
| Hospital based | 72 | 29 | 34.82% | 30.89% | 0.14% | 181.22% |

*From The Health Care Group's *The Goodwill Registry Year 2001*. Figures reflect average values from 1990 – 2001 and illustrate a percentage of the practice's gross revenue. HCG drops the "zero" values and average all those reported in a given specialty. HCG compiles this registry each year and the data prove most helpful when practices compare individual listings that match their specific geographic location. However, we provide the averages as general benchmarks. Contact HCG at (800) 473-0032 about obtaining a copy of the Registry.

✓ A trained work force including physicians and support staff

✓ Effective billing, information, collecting and scheduling systems

✓ Non-compete covenants with member physicians

*Practice* goodwill implicitly includes the value of having an established patient base and current and transferable referral patterns from which to establish immediate and substantial cash flow, *regardless of what specific physicians* do the work. Our box above offers a simplified example of this kind of "going concern" value.

*"Personal"* goodwill — future income that depends on an individual physician's reputation and continued practice — is a different story. If a particular physician's departure will decimate the patient base, his/her personal goodwill adds no salable value.

Goodwill somewhat reflects the cost of putting a practice together from scratch according to Pavarini. A brand new practice can't generate the same revenue as an established one, so goodwill includes the difference between actual and potential revenue during the start-up period.

> ## Calculating 'Going Concern' Value
>
> Publisher and ex-consultant Leif Beck offers the following example illustrating real dollar value arising from *practice* goodwill. Suppose the following:
>
> In ABCD Urology Group, each of the four urologists receives $240,000 in annual salary plus a $30,000 retirement contribution. In their well-integrated practice, patients and referrers know that any of the four doctors can expertly handle their concerns.
>
> With this kind of group strength, ABCD Urology's gross income will probably remain about the same even if Dr. A retires and is replaced by "Dr. New." The group would probably pay Dr. New a $120,000 starting salary (with no first-year retirement contribution), leaving Drs. B, C and D with an extra $150,000 of profit the first year. In the second year, Dr. New's salary might typically become $160,000 (plus $30,000 to retirement), leaving the seniors an extra $80,000; and so on for several more years.
>
> What, asks Beck, are those extra earnings if not the practice's goodwill value?

## So what's it worth?

Hanging a price tag on goodwill continues to puzzle even the experts today. Some advisors use a "discounted cash flow" technique that depends heavily on *predictable* future earnings. But "predictable" hardly describes today's health care economics!

On the other hand, a "market value" or "comparable sales" approach may provide the most reliable method.

The benchmarks in the HCG *Goodwill Registry* provide nothing more than a starting point. Don't simply refer to the data and assume your practice is worth the top of the reported range for your specialty. Too many individual factors greatly affect your actual value. Factors that can make a huge difference include:

- Overall profitability and economic soundness
- Practice location
- Competition

- Managed care success
- Ancillary revenue and service diversity
- Local population and economic trends
- Referral patterns (for specialty practices)
- Payor mix
- Non-compete covenants (for group practices)

## The More Things Change....

In the early 90's, nervousness over the future of private medicine prompted many experts to predict eroding goodwill values. But, in spite of all the doomsday talk, reported goodwill values remained fairly consistent with those from 10-plus years ago — averaging around 30% of gross practice revenue.

In the recent past, some hospitals, PPMCs and other institutions offered breathtaking amounts for goodwill — especially for some primary care practices. Those days may be over, but goodwill lives on as a calculable asset. Don't allow a potential buyer or merger partner to assign an arbitrary number and call it "goodwill." Insist on a thorough evaluation that takes into account comparable sales adjusted by what makes your practice unique.

### The reality check

Attorney and consultant Bernick says you should subject your finally determined goodwill/receivables figure (the amount justifying the separation pay) to this reality check:

> Assume that one senior partner retires and you hire a young replacement physician. If the practice retains 70-90% of the retiring member's patient volume, which it should be able to do, will it have enough revenue to pay both the new doctor's salary and benefits (initially lower than those of the retiree) and the departed doctor's pay-out? If so, the group can afford the pay-out without reducing the remaining members' incomes.

Many practices find that 12 months' continued salary (spread over a longer time period) represents a reasonable pay-out in terms of goodwill value and accounts receivable. Carefully scrutinize payouts substantially deviating from that mark. It may be too onerous for the practice if the prospects for continuing its level of profitability truly are doubtful.

**Avoid doomsday talk**

Don't get caught up in the doomsday fears that private medical practice is going to hell in a hand-basket. While it's fine to take into account highly probable future adverse events, you can protect yourself against broadly worrisome scenarios by imposing special conditions that enable you to be fair (and not ultraconservative) to a retiring member without putting the continuing partners at risk.

Your best tactic: Spread the payments over three to five years, but subject them to a well-defined percentage limitation based on *net* income. Include a cushion of a few extra years to handle unpaid excess, but establish an absolute drop-dead date. Such a course allows a retiring partner a fair pay-out and ongoing members a reasonable escape hatch.

**Protect the group**

To protect the ongoing group — and by extension the departing partner — the practice's continued financial health must be of paramount concern. It's shortsighted for any partner to expect a very large pay-out that disregards the group's ongoing finances.

For starters, no one knows which partner will be the first to qualify for payments. A weary senior member may look forward to retiring first, but a much younger partner might die or quit before that. In any event, it never makes sense to kill the goose that lays the golden egg. For tax reasons, deferred compensation is rarely secured by collateral. Thus, a retiring doctor may have difficulty collecting an agreed but excessive pay-out from hard-pressed colleagues.

**Pick the time period**

So first make sure to spread the pay-out over a reasonable number of years — ideally three to five. Shorter periods may put undue pressure on the continuing partners' incomes, whereas a longer period denies them psychological closure on the obligation and a relief from its drag on current earnings.

This time period also allows you to limit payment if the departed member soon competes with his/her old practice. No one likes to pay a former colleague turned competitor. Paying too quickly means the ex-member has nothing to lose by competing.

Next, combine the period with a dollar limit based on the remaining members' continuing ability to afford these payments. Bernick sometimes recommends keying simply to the practice's annual gross revenues. If post-termination receipts fall, then perhaps departed members' payments should decrease as well. Some contracts thus call for the payments to decrease if in any year they exceed a stated percentage (sometimes 5%) of that year's gross income.

### Tie it to net income

One problem with that approach: Percentage-of-gross limitations reflect top line revenue and ignore the important bottom line. Yet some physicians correctly note that rising overhead poses an equal threat to their finances. Even if set very low, the gross income limit still leaves many younger physicians feeling uneasy. They want assurance that their incomes won't be cut to fund a former colleague's retirement.

While the two sides' financial interests naturally oppose each other, guaranteeing salary puts all the risk on the departed doctor and none on the practice. Thus Bernick instead proposes changing the percentage of gross limits to a percentage of net.

But define net income carefully to prevent misunderstandings about what counts against income for this purpose. Generally, net income should mean gross revenue minus all expenses *except* physician compensation items: doctors' salaries, bonuses, retirement plan contributions and possibly their auto expenses, CME costs, entertainment, dues and journals.

### Reasonable risk

The main problem with the net income approach: It's more complicated to calculate than the gross income limit. Furthermore, it may leave a departed member uneasy about expenses being misclassified in order to reduce the pay-out. Remedy this problem with careful contract definitions and by allowing a departed doctor to audit the practice's calculations.

To be sure, a departed partner bears more risk under the net income limit, since s/he is subject to ongoing risk on both revenue and overhead. However, it seems reasonable for the senior to bear both these risks, since rising overhead is just as legitimate a business risk as decreasing receipts.

## Establish a firm extension

What if the limit actually comes into play because part of the annual payment exceeds the stated percentage of that year's income? First of all, if several departed members are receiving payments, most contracts reduce their amounts either equally or proportionately until the total falls within the limit.

Still, unpaid excess is possible. In that case, carry it to succeeding years in which practice finances hopefully improve enough to allow catch-up without violating the limit. But establish a drop-dead date that extinguishes the obligation even if the finances do not improve.

The following paragraph provides a sample contract provision along those lines. But note that this sample is for illustration only and is not complete. Consult with your attorney for language fleshing out one's proportionate share, how the pay-out should be reduced, obtaining the former partner's reimbursement regardless of separation pay, etc.

*Any payment reduced hereunder [by the percentage limit] shall be payable in continued monthly installments due in the succeeding year or years, subject along with any regularly required payments to the continuing [percentage] limit, but the total period for such make-up payments shall not extend longer than an additional twenty-four (24) months, after which no further amounts shall be payable.*

# Advance Provisions for Special Situations

In addition to limiting payments to a stated percentage of the group's income (gross or net), you may want to build in protection against six other circumstances that may make the pay-out unaffordable. Here's what to do:

**1** *When several partners depart at once.* You may be able to afford generous monthly payments if one member dies, retires or withdraws. But what if a second and, God forbid, even a third partner leaves shortly thereafter? To protect the group, consider a provision reducing the pay-out by one-third if there are two concurrent absences and perhaps by half (or even more) in case three or more doctors leave.

Consider extending the payment period if this reduction comes into play. After all, it's probably not the first departed partner's fault that another member dies, becomes disabled or quits. Consider continuing the payments for an extra month for each month they are reduced, but not longer than it takes to end up with the same total pay-out amount.

**2** *When liabilities arise after departure.* Suppose several months after a partner's departure a Medicare audit finds billing errors that occurred while s/he was a member. Or a malpractice claim is filed that may result in group liability above insurance limits. Or the IRS assesses back taxes based on deductions that have benefited all group members? Should the departed partner avoid sharing in these obligations because they failed to ripen before s/he left?

Some groups decide they should, exempting a member from claims arising after s/he leaves the group in the belief that no one should have to fear the past after a clean departure. Others feel that a partner should not profit from group activities and then escape costs when the piper comes to be paid. While both views are reasonable, Bernick prefers the latter — at least for liabilities arising a year or two after departure.

If that's your view, here is sample language that subjects the pay-out to such a "lookback:"

> *If any claim(s) are asserted against [the practice] for activities occurring before a member's departure, whether arising out of alleged malpractice, third-party reimbursement, tax deficiencies or otherwise, the separation pay shall be reduced by his/her proportionate share of the financial responsibility therefore.*

3 *When a partner received sick pay prior to departure.* Suppose a member was absent due to illness, presumably receiving considerable sick pay, and then dies or retires shortly thereafter. Bernick suggests inserting a provision reducing a member's separation pay by any pay or income share received while out sick, unless the member has been back to full-time work for a specified period of time.

4 *When notice is short.* What if a member announces withdrawal effective in two weeks, perhaps to take a new and immediate position? Your group may not have the time to recruit a replacement doctor or otherwise restructure itself to cover the absence. Consider inserting a penalty like one-sixth of the pay-out for each month less than six that a departing member fails to give notice of intent to withdraw.

5 *When benefits carry forward.* Suppose you have just paid a year's malpractice premium when your partner leaves to practice in another part of the state — using the same coverage. Fairness calls for offsetting benefits like malpractice, life, health or disability insurance premiums, professional society dues and even auto usage to the extent they benefit your departed member after the departure date.

6 *When a departed doctor competes with you.* It just makes no sense to pay a withdrawing member for the goodwill value left behind if the ex-partner uses that goodwill for his/her own benefit elsewhere. So be sure your document reduces or eliminates the pay-out if the withdrawing member enters practice in your specialty in your service area while receiving the payments.

Managed care makes this concern more real than ever. Suppose your group has a contract covering many of an HMO's members. You can hardly afford to pay an ex-partner if s/he contracts with the HMO for many of those same lives. Good documents these days specifically prohibit contracting with managed care plans serviced by the group.

While some physicians still argue that it is unprofessional to restrict someone from competing, a pay-out limitation is somewhat different. It leaves the doctor free to compete, only denying separation pay in that event. Despite this difference, do not set up any such condition without legal advice. In some states courts will not enforce it.

# Acknowledgements

As Publisher, I am proud to see this book on medical practice partnerships come to fruition. We took our previous book on the subject and considerably updated it to current conditions, adding new ideas and text in the process. All of us at Advisory Publications expect this effort will benefit you greatly.

Special credit goes first to Teresa Norris, senior editor of our *Orthopedic Practice Advisor* and *Group Practice Solutions* newsletters. She revised, compiled and wrote the bulk of this book. It was a job well done.

Tim Boden, our senior editor of *The Physician's Advisory*, wrote chapter 3, dealing with physician leadership. Tim has a strong interest in the subject of leadership in medical practice, which I think you'll detect in that text.

Finally, no writing project ever goes well unless someone undertakes to coordinate and lead the writers' efforts. Our senior editor for ancillary products, Janis Bucsko, undertook that responsibility, keeping the project moving to a timely finish while insisting on quality work.

Special thanks go, too, to the many fine professionals listed below, whose sharp insights and good advice you'll find throughout this book.

Leif C. Beck
Publisher

**Geoffrey T. Anders**, The Health Care Group, Plymouth Meeting, PA; (610) 828-3888; fax (610) 828-3658; e-mail to *ganders@healthcaregroup.com*.

**Randy Bauman**, Delta Healthcare in Brentwood, TN; (800) 467-3310; fax (614) 377-0270; e-mail to *rb@deltahealthcare.com*.

**Daniel M. Bernick**, The Health Care Group, Plymouth Meeting, PA; (610) 828-3888; fax (610) 828-3658; e-mail to *dbernick@healthcaregroup.com*.

**Robert Bohlmann**, FACMPE, MGMA Consulting Services; (817) 461-8607; e-mail to *consulting@mgma.com*.

**Susan Cejka**, formerly with Cejka & Co., St. Louis; (800) 678-78588-7858; fax (314) 726-1603; online at *www.cejka.com*.

**Janice G. Cunningham**, The Health Care Group, Plymouth Meeting, PA; (610) 828-3888; fax (610) 828-3658; e-mail to *jcunningham@healthcaregroup.com*.

**Tracy Duberman**, Hay Group; (201) 557-8400; fax (201) 557-8444; e-mail to *tracy_duberman@haygroup.com*.

**L. Michael Fleischman**, principal with Gates, Moore & Company; (404) 266-9876; fax (404) 266-2669; email to *mfleischman@gatesmoore.com*.

**Richard C. Haines, Jr.**, Medical Design International in Tucker, GA; (770) 939-7950; fax (770) 939-7522; e-mail to *haines@mdiatlanta.com*.

**Jeri Harris, CPH-C**, former coding consultant and now with Charleston Orthopedic; (843) 769-2000; fax (843) 769-2260; e-mail to *JeriLynn48@aol.com*.

**Bruce Johnson, JD, MPA,** MGMA Consulting Services; (888) 608-5601; ext. 877; e-mail to *consulting@mgma.com*.

**Vasilios J. (Bill) Kalogredis**, Kalogredis, Tsoulis & Sweeney, Ltd., Wayne, PA; (610) 795-8314; fax (610) 687-8402.

**Keith M. Korenchuk**, partner in the health law section of Davis, Wright, Tremaine, LLP in Charlotte, NC; (704) 332-0800; Fax (704) 332-0799; e-mail to *keithkorenchuk@dwt.com*.

**Mitchell D. Kusy, PhD.**, author and professor at the University of St. Thomas, Minneapolis, MN; (651) 962-4530; fax (651) 962-4810; e-mail to *mekusy@stthomas.edu*.

**J. Thomas Martin**, Health Care Management Consulting and Project Development; (205) 733-1202; fax (205) 733-8340; e-mail to *tkjtm@earthlink.net*.

**Sandra D. McGraw**, The Health Care Group, Plymouth Meeting, PA; (610) 828-3888; fax (610) 828-3658; e-mail to *smcgraw@healthcaregroup.com*.

**Kevin McWhorter, CPA**, (now deceased), of McWhorter & Co., in Akron, OH.

**Robert A. Nelson, FACMPE**, Principal, Canon Gorup LLC; (805) 682-3913; fax (805) 682-3923; e-mail to *ransbarb@aol.com*.

**Michael J. Parshall**, The Health Care Group, Plymouth Meeting, PA; (610) 828-3888; fax (610) 828-3658; e-mail to *mparshall@healthcaregroup.com*.

**Peter A. Pavarini**, Schottenstein, Zox & Dunn; (614) 462-5016; fax (614) 464-1135; e-mail to *ppavarini@szd.com*.

**John-Henry Pfifferling**, Center for Professional Well-Being in Durham, NC; (919) 489-9167; fax (919) 419-0011; e-mail to *cpwb@mindspring.com*.

**James M. Ramsey**, James M. Ramsey & Associates, Jacksonville, FL; (904) 321-0350; fax (904) 321-0370.

**David N. Shipman**, Integrated Strategies, Overland Park, KS; (913) 649-0080; fax (913) 649-0532; e-mail *dshipman@prgusa.com*.

**Paul W. Smith**, CPBC. The Health Care Group, Plymouth Meeting, PA; (610) 828-3888; fax (610) 828-3658; e-mail to *psmith@healthcaregroup.com*.

**Dorothy R. Sweeney**, formerly of the Health Care Group and now Editorial Directory for Advisory Publications; (888) 941-4488; fax (610) 941-4499; e-mail to *dsweeney@advisorypub.com*.

**Gary W. Thompson**, Rocky Mountain Professional Consultants Inc., Lakewood, CO; (303) 239-6100; fax (303) 239-0560; e-mail to *ThompsonGW@aol.com*.

**James W. Tripp**, The Schenck Health Services Group, Appleton, WI; (920) 731-8112; fax (920) 739-0124; e-mail to *trippj@schenckcpa.com*.

**J. Gray Tuttle Jr**., Professional Consultants, Inc., Lansing, MI; (517) 372-7611; fax (517) 372-2770; e-mail to *gtuttle@rrpc.com*.

**Jack Valancy**, Jack Valancy Consulting, Cleveland Heights, OH; (216) 721-8990; (216) 721-6825; e-mail to *jack@valancy.com*.

**Robert A. Wade**, Wade, Goldstein, London and Abruzzo, PC; (610) 296-1800; e-mail to *RWad@wadegold.com*.

**Bette Warn, CMPE**, Woodridge Orthopaedic and Spine Center, Wheat Ridge, CO; (303) 422-1388, ext. 3310; fax (303) 422-3422; e-mail to *bwarn@mho.com*.

# Check out these other products from Advisory Publications — designed to improve your practice's success!

**Group Practice Solutions:** Our newsletter dedicated to addressing the specific partner-level issues of group medical practices. *GPS* offers practical, real-life ways to solve difficult issues such as: income division, partner buy-in and pay-out agreements, physician leadership, dealing with difficult partners, handling a partner's special request, and more. *[12 monthly issues for $149.]*

***The Physician's Advisory®:*** Our flagship newsletter, in print for over 24 years. *The Physician's Advisory* touches on all aspects of effectively running a more profitable and efficient medical practice. Rely on *The Physician's Advisory* for in-depth coverage of ways to address and improve your practice's financial management, personnel management, partner-level matters, practice marketing, reimbursement improvement, and more. *[12 monthly issues for $149.]*

**Staff Management Strategies for Medical Offices:** A monthly newsletter focused on giving physicians and managers the strategies, insight, data and *proven* techniques they need to build, train and maintain a top-performing office staff. Learn sure-fire methods for: hiring the right person the *first* time; motivating, compensating and retaining top-notch staff; using your existing staff more effectively; and more. *[12 monthly issues for $149.]*

**Financial Management Strategies for Medical Offices:** Each monthly issue provides tools and advice you can use to improve financial controls, boost managed plan profitability, deal with partner-level financial disputes effectively, make informed decisions about your practice's long-range planning, track and manage your receivables, do cost-benefit analyses, and more. *[12 monthly issues for $149.]*

### 100% Money-back ANYTIME GUARANTEE

If <u>at</u> <u>any</u> <u>time</u> during your subscription you decide our publication is not helping you improve your practice, just tell us and we'll refund your <u>entire</u> one-year subscription payment. Even if you've received 11 of your 12 issues. No hassles. No problems. Guaranteed.

**(TO ORDER, please use the form on the reverse side of this page)**

# Order Form — Special Discount for New Subscribers!

| Publication | List Price | You Save! | Your Price | Qty. | Total |
|---|---|---|---|---|---|
| Group Practice Solutions | $299 | 50% | $149 | | |
| The Physician's Advisory® | $279 | 47% | $149 | | |
| Staff Management Strategies for Medical Offices | $199 | 25% | $149 | | |
| Financial Management Strategies for Medical Offices | $299 | 50% | $149 | | |
| | | | | Total | |

## 3 Easy Ways To Order!
1. Fax the completed form with payment to **610-941-4499**.
2. Call toll-free to order **888-941-4488**.
3. Mail the completed form along with payment to:
   **Advisory Publications**
   **15 E. Ridge Pike, Suite 510**
   **Conshohocken, PA 19428**

## Payment & Shipping
❏ My check is enclosed (payable to Advisory Publications)
❏ Please charge my credit card:
   ❏ Visa   ❏ MasterCard   ❏ American Express

Account Number:_____

Exp. Date: _____

Signature:_____

Name:_____

Address:_____

_____

City:_____ State:_____ Zip:_____

Phone: (_____)_____ Fax: (_____)_____

E-mail:_____

**For a complete listing of all our newsletters, books, audio tapes, and special reports, visit our website at www.AdvisoryPublications.com**

PBOC601